the Final mile

the Final mile

A wife's response
to her husband's terminal illness

Faye Landrum

Tyndale House Publishers, Inc.
WHEATON, ILLINOIS

Library of Congress Cataloging-in-Publication Data

Landrum, Faye.
    The final mile : God's presence in cancer's final fight : helping caregivers cope / Faye Landrum.
        p.   cm.
    Includes bibliographical references.
    ISBN 0-8423-3483-1 (sc. : alk. paper)
        1. Caregivers—Religious life.   2. Terminal care—Religious aspects—Christianity.   3. Landrum, Faye.   4. Cancer—Patients—Care—United States—Case studies.   5. Cancer—Religious aspects—Christianity.   I. Title.
BV4910.9.L35   1999
248.8'621—dc21   99-039696

Printed in the United States of America

03   02   01   00   99

6   5   4   3   2   1

Table of Contents

Preface
Acknowledgments

Preface

This book is about the last six months of my husband's battle with cancer. It is also the story of my stress, how the pressures molded me, and how God helped me over the rough spots. My prayer is that my sharing this with you will help soften some of those rough spots so inevitable for anyone caring for a terminally ill loved one.

My experiences may be quite different from yours, but at the end of the book in "Caregiver Concerns," I have listed suggestions that may help with many problems all caregivers face sooner or later. I have tried to envision us having a friendly chat over a cup of tea, mutually discussing our difficulties and helping each other.

Faye Landrum

Acknowledgments

My sincere thanks to:

My pastor, Donald Davies, for patiently reading each installment of the manuscript and helping me with my computer problems

My lawyer, Dean Smith, for his legal expertise

My hospice nurse, Gail Kubick, for advice regarding the professional care of terminally ill patients

Mark Sebastian for his knowledge pertaining to Social Security

Dorothy Cain for her help with banking procedures

Bonnie and Tom Haralson, whose love and friendship sustained me through the long days of my husband's illness, and for Bonnie's help later in preparing the book manuscript

Mona Hodgson and Marlene Bagnull for their editorial expertise

Phyllis Yoders of the Area Agency on Aging, for information on available programs

Dave Richard for help in understanding welfare programs

Dick McNary for his assistance with alternative health treatments

PART ONE

My Story

What and Who

Mine is not just to write
the what of my darkest night,
but Who was there to provide His light.[1]

By Elaine Creasman

---

[1] Elaine Creasman, "What and Who," *The Christian Communicator* (August 1994). Used by permission of Elaine Creasman.

Chapter 1

An Ominous Cloud

Cast all your anxiety on him because he cares for you.
1 PETER 5:7, NIV

When your loved one has a terminal illness, it hurts. I know—I've
been there.

The Thursday before Easter, I drove my husband to the hospital
outpatient department for radiation treatment on his arm, where a new
tumor had recently developed. My sullen mood almost matched the
dark April sky. Even the anticipation of our family's coming to visit
didn't lessen my awareness of Bob's worsening illness.

I walked around to the passenger side to help Bob out of the car.
The cancer had affected his legs. Dejectedly he lifted up his right
thigh with both hands and swung his legs out to the pavement. He
struggled to get a sure footing, then firmly placed his hand on my
shoulder to start walking. Too proud to use a cane, he used me for
his support.

Over the past six months progressive numbness had afflicted his
right leg, making him unsteady. After falling several times, he was
constantly plagued by fear of falling. Together we walked into the
hospital and down the corridor to radiation therapy.

"My back hurts worse than my arm today," Bob muttered. "Maybe they ought to radiate my back instead of my arm."

"Ask the doctor about it," I replied. Consulting the doctor was my stock remedy in medical matters. Recently there didn't seem to be any other solution.

For eleven years Bob had battled multiple myeloma—bone cancer. Knowing that longevity usually ranged from three to five years after diagnosis, we were thankful for that extended time. But as Easter approached, an ominous feeling nagged at me that this might be our last one together. Time seemed to be running out. If I let myself think about it, panic rose within me like an incoming tide. How could I ever handle the inevitable?

When Bob had first become ill more than a decade ago, we had no hint that cancer was invading his body. A persistent, worsening back-ache took him to several doctors, but X rays confirmed their diagnosis of osteoarthritis. While playing golf at a company outing, he felt such pain in his back that he could go no farther than the fifth hole. The next day excruciating pain kept him confined to bed.

Later a doctor put him in the hospital. A CAT scan revealed a tumor the size of an orange on the underside of his pelvic bone. Conventional X rays had not detected it. Further tests and a bone-marrow sample confirmed the diagnosis of bone cancer.

Bob's doctor told him the news. That afternoon during visiting hours, Bob told me.

"I know now why my back aches," he said from his hospital bed.

"Why?" I asked, pulling a chair up next to him. When I sat down, I reached for his hand.

"I have bone cancer. The doctor just told me. All the tests proved it."

At the mention of the word *cancer,* I felt as if someone had dumped ice water down my back. All strength drained from me, and I put my head down on his chest and cried. Bob gently laid his hand on my shoulder.

When I regained my composure, I asked, "What do we do now?" My throat was parched and my eyes hurt.

"The doctor said an oncologist will be in to see me," Bob said.

"Will you have to take chemotherapy?"

"I don't know. I suppose the doctor will tell me."

We talked more about the prospects; then Bob handed me the get-well cards that had come that day. I wasn't interested in seeing them, but I realized he was trying to bolster my spirits by showing them to me. And I tried to appear brave to encourage him.

When I left to go home that evening, my nerves were frayed, and I couldn't find the ticket to the hospital parking deck. I told the attendant, "My husband has just been diagnosed with cancer. I don't know where anything is."

The attendant smiled sympathetically. "It's OK. Just go on home," he said as he raised the bar to let my car out.

Bob came home two days later. His tumor caused pressure on his sciatic nerve. His pain was so intense that he felt as if his leg were on fire. Lying flat in bed with no pressure on his back or pelvis provided a modicum of relief and comfort. Sitting in a chair was torture. He was forced to eat his meals lying flat. For twenty-one days I helped him struggle into the car to go to the hospital for daily radiation treatments. With the seat laid back almost flat, he could tolerate the ride. The doctor started him on chemotherapy, which consisted of a four-day regimen of pills to be taken every four to six weeks. Fortunately the treatment did not make him sick or cause loss of hair.

As a nurse, I worked at our local hospital on the afternoon shift. Before I left for work, I prepared Bob's supper and left it in the oven with the timer set. He had a phone by his bed, and I checked on him frequently.

Radiation eased his pain, and chemotherapy shrank the cancer. By the end of summer, he had improved enough that he went back to his job as a chemist in the adhesive division of BF Goodrich. By Christmas he was nearly pain free. Our lives almost returned to a precancerous routine—with moderate activity restriction.

Every few months, however, a new lesion—or tumor as we called it—would develop in another bone. Thus the term *multiple myeloma.* Radiation usually eased the resulting pain.

Near that last Easter when Bob and I went into the hospital for the last radiation treatment on his arm, the receptionist greeted him warmly. After eleven years, everyone knew him on a first-name basis.

"How's it going today?" the receptionist asked.

"Not too good," Bob replied. "I'm having a lot more trouble with my back. Can I see the doctor today?" Usually a radiologist was on duty and willing to see any patient with a problem.

"The doctor's not here today," she replied, "but I can schedule a visit on Tuesday."

"That will be fine," Bob said, then together we walked to the changing room, where I helped him put on a hospital gown.

On the way home we talked about our family's coming to visit us for the Easter weekend. Gary, our younger son, was coming from Columbus, Ohio. He is a corporate pilot and did not get to visit often. Gary would bring Dana, his new girlfriend, with him. I was delighted to learn she was a Christian. Steve would be coming from Los Angeles with his wife, Laura, and their three children: Zachary, who was nine; Gwendolyn, age four; and two-year-old Charity, who from birth had been nicknamed "Kit."

That weekend was filled with the laughter of grandchildren. Before everyone departed, we took a family picture using an automatic timer. Later, I was glad we did. It proved to be our last one.

Bob enjoyed the children, but the confusion tired him. He chose to stay home from church that Sunday and rest. His back pained him too much to sit in a rigid pew.

He watched an Easter service on TV while the rest of us went to church. The resurrection sermon was especially meaningful to me. The message reminded me of the precious promise of God's presence.

After supper Sunday night Bob watched the children playing, but he was restless and in some pain. He announced he wanted to go to bed.

"I sure hope the doctor can give me some relief on Tuesday," Bob said as I kissed him good night. That was my hope, too.

No cloud is so dark that the Son cannot penetrate it.

Chapter 2

Hope in Hopelessness

*[Jesus said], "In my house are many mansions: . . .
I go to prepare a place for you."*
JOHN 14:2

Monday morning, as I watched Bob struggle to get out of bed with the help of a cane, I cautiously suggested that a hospital bed might help him.

"How about calling hospice for some help?" I asked. "Maybe they could supply a hospital bed for you."

"Isn't hospice for people who are dying?"

"I know it's for people who need care," I responded, avoiding the gloom of his question.

"OK," Bob said, "go ahead and call them."

I phoned Bob's oncologist to ask his opinion. He readily agreed and said he would contact hospice for us. Later that day we made arrangements for a hospice representative to come to the house the following afternoon.

Early Tuesday morning, Bob and I went to the hospital for his date with the doctor. "I sure hope more radiation will help my back," he said as we walked down the corridor to radiation therapy. His limp was more obvious now, and he leaned heavily on my shoulder.

When the doctor came into the examining room, Bob immediately told him about his back problem.

"I've been reviewing your file," the doctor said, "and I am afraid we can't give any more radiation to your back."

"Why not?" Bob gasped, as if he had been slapped.

"You've had too much radiation to that area. If we give you any more, you may be much worse off than you are now."

Since first diagnosed with cancer, Bob had received numerous radiation treatments to his lower back.

"What would happen if I got more radiation?" Bob asked.

"It might cause permanent diarrhea or an open sore that wouldn't heal."

"Isn't there anything you can do to relieve the pain?"

"I can give you pain medication," the doctor answered. He scrawled out a prescription for Dilaudid, a narcotic analgesic, to be taken every four hours. "I'm sorry," he said as he handed it to Bob.

Silence filled the car on our way home. I searched for words that might help. What do you say when an insurmountable mountain looms ahead? We both knew the mountain was there, but neither of us knew how to talk about it.

That afternoon Gail, the hospice representative, came to our home. Steve and Laura, who were still visiting us, discreetly left the house, taking the children with them.

As we sat around the dining room table, Gail asked Bob about his diagnosis and what problems he was having. She explained that hospice gives care to patients with limited life expectancy. "Our purpose is to promote comfort, relieve physical symptoms and emotional strain," Gail said, "and encourage independence as much as possible. Most medical equipment is supplied, and a nurse stops by at least twice a week."

Bob had no questions. Then she said softly, "The state of Ohio requires that I ask you if you have a living will and a durable power of attorney. Without a living will you would be subjected to any procedure necessary to keep you living. The durable power of attorney appoints an advocate to make decisions for you if you are not able."

Bob acknowledged he had both those legal documents. We had mutually decided long before that we wanted no heroic treatments.

"Are you aware that paramedics do not honor living wills?" Gail asked. When Bob said he didn't know that, Gail showed us a paper that would ensure that no extraordinary measures would be used by paramedics. It would be Bob's request not to be resuscitated. Not an easy paper to sign, but he did it.

Gail looked directly into Bob's eyes. "If you agree to just comfort care with no aggressive treatment, then we can help you, and you will have benefits under Medicare through hospice that pay for all medications. This means you will not be receiving chemotherapy, radiation, or anything to effect a cure for your illness."

I watched Bob's expression. Only *comfort* care. His disease was terminal. He would not recover. Being hit with such devastating news twice in the same day was almost more than we could cope with. I felt a wave of despair wash over me. Bob had fought so hard for his health. And now we knew for sure it was terminal.

Over the past eleven years, in addition to traditional medical treatments, Bob had tried alternative treatments: miso soup, high potency mineral supplements, herb powders, and acupuncture. It was not easy to accept the fact that there was now nothing more to be tried.

Bob looked down at the floor, and his shoulders slumped a little as he agreed to have only "comfort care."

After Gail left, Steve, Laura, and the grandchildren came back into the house. "Are they going to bring the hospital bed?" Steve asked.

"Yes—and they are going to have a nurse come by twice a week to check on Daddy," I said, trying to appear cheerful.

"That sounds like a good idea to me," Laura pronounced as she tried to interest the children in a new construction project with blocks.

Bob watched the children a few minutes. I realized he was probably thinking he might never see them again. Finally he said in a restrained voice, "But I can't continue with chemotherapy if I am getting hospice care."

"Why not?" Steve and Laura asked in unison.

"Because they give care only to the terminally ill." This was the first time Bob had said the words *terminally ill*. They hung in the air. No one knew what to say.

I cupped my hands over Bob's to communicate my love. "It looks like heaven is my next stop," he said softly, his eyes downcast. Then he turned to me and added, "Maybe that isn't too bad a place to be."

The prospect of heaven opened the way for further conversation as Steve said facetiously, "Check up on those streets of gold for us, Gampi."

That night we talked more about the hope that is above all hopelessness: the hope of heaven—a wonderful place, a prepared place for those who have trusted Jesus as Savior.

As Emily Dickinson wrote in her poem, "This World Is Not Conclusion":

> *This world is not conclusion;*
> *a sequel stands beyond,*
> *Invisible, as music,*
> *but positive as sound.*

Positive as sound! What an encouragement!

My Daily Devotional Calendar said it another way: "Some may see a hopeless end, but as believers we rejoice in an endless hope."[1]

I was so thankful for that hope, but after we went to bed that night and I was alone in the dark, I wasn't quite so confident. Tears moistened my cheeks as I thought about the frightening future. God seemed a long way off. How could I reach Him?

I remembered being scared on a cold, snowy night when I was a lit-

[1]From *Bless Your Heart.* Used by permission of Heartland Samplers, Inc. Copyright © 1990.

tle girl, no more than five years old. I was in a car with my father. We had to go up a steep, slippery hill. With the wheels spinning on the ice, the car made it only halfway up the incline. My dad said he had to back down the hill, and I was frantic with fear. Then I looked over to my dad, and a small sense of peace returned. Nothing could be hazardous with my strong father beside me. Was not my heavenly Father beside me now?

I visualized Jesus standing by my bed. Two verses of Scripture came to my mind as I drifted off to sleep: "Come near to God and he will come near to you" (James 4:8, NIV); "I do believe; help me overcome my unbelief!" (Mark 9:24, NIV).

The next day hospice delivered a hospital bed to our home. Steve dismantled the twin bed that Bob always slept in and stored it in the attic. The new bed fit easily into our bedroom beside mine.

Along with the bed, the delivery men also brought a walker. In the last two days Bob had agreed to use a cane in the house, but I doubted he would accept the walker. It would be just one more step closer to the loss of independence. Yet he didn't resist learning how to use it.

The walker helped prevent Bob from falling and gave him an added sense of security. He manipulated it through the living room and kitchen to the back door. He stopped at the step that led down onto the patio.

Steve and I watched his progress. When Bob seemed stymied by the step, Steve said, "Wait, Dad, maybe there's something in the shed that will help."

Steve went to the metal shed in the backyard and found a few cement blocks. He put the blocks in front of the kitchen step; they were exactly the same height as the step. The step was wide enough for the feet of Bob's walker. He could then easily come outside to the glassed-in patio and to the backyard beyond. Two cement blocks had created a small gateway to freedom.

I didn't realize it then, but those cement blocks were the first of many provisions that God would supply over the next six months. Our faith would be tested and our trust stretched to the breaking point, but always we would find that God was there to strengthen us and to provide for our needs. Sometimes He used little ordinary things like cement blocks as the solution. Sometimes His help was spiritual in nature.

As we considered the odyssey ahead, God's promises became more precious to us—especially the promise of eternal life.

Heaven is home with a paid-up mortgage.

Chapter 3

Tested Trust

What time I am afraid, I will trust in thee.
PSALM 56:3

A few days after Steve and Laura left for California with the children, Gail came to the house for the start of her biweekly visits. When she went into the bedroom where Bob was waiting for her, he greeted her warmly. "Nurse Gail," he said, "it's good to see you again."

She laughed at the salutation. The term, "Nurse Gail," seemed to fit her well. As she checked his blood pressure and listened to his lungs with her stethoscope, she put him at ease with casual conversation.

Her warm personality and compassion made me thankful she was part of Bob's health care. Her visit, however, made me realize anew that the reason for her coming was the terminal nature of his ill-ness—and suddenly panic gripped me.

Whenever I thought about the future, my mouth became dry and my chest hurt. Bob knew he was going to be with the Lord—but what about me? Widowhood meant being left behind to face the future alone, and the prospect scared me.

Could I maintain a car by myself without knowing anything about oil changes and tire pressures? And what about the house? Even changing a lightbulb was a challenge for me. Bob always took care of such matters.

During the day, I could handle my apprehension quite well. The myriad of things needing to be done occupied my time and controlled my mind. Bob's needs had to be cared for. The house had to be cleaned, groceries bought, meals prepared, bills paid, letters written, and the phone answered.

At night, when the house was dark, fear clutched me. What would I do if the washing machine broke down—or the garage door wouldn't go up? Some of my fears were irrational, but in the dark silence they were very real to me.

One night I awoke from a restless sleep, and the words of a song by Bill Gaither came to mind:

> *Because He lives I can face tomorrow,*
> *Because He lives all fear is gone;*
> *Because I know He holds the future.*
> *And life is worth the living just because He lives.*[1]

I had heard it recently at church. The reassurance of those words was like a personal message from God. Yes, I could face the future because the *living* God was with me.

Hadn't He promised in Matthew 28:20 that He would never leave us? So why was I afraid? That song reminded me of this verse of Scripture, and it was like a warm blanket on a cold night.

The next day I found the words of the song printed in our church bulletin. I cut them out and taped them to the letter holder on the desk in the living room. Every time I sat at the desk to talk on the phone, write a check, or pen a letter, those words were in front of me. They reminded me that God was with me, and together we could handle the future.

Whenever I looked out the kitchen window and noticed a bird hopping about in the backyard, God's feathered creatures also reassured

[1] Words by William J. & Gloria Gaither. Music by William J. Gaither. ©1971 William J. Gaither ASCAP. All rights reserved. Used by permission.

me of His presence. If an insignificant little sparrow doesn't fall without our Lord taking note of it (Matthew 10:29), certainly He was aware of my problems, too.

I often repeated to anyone harboring a concern, "When you get to the river, God will build the bridge." Gary was about twelve years old when he heard me say that one day.

"And don't make rivers that aren't there," he added.

Don't make rivers that aren't there! Wasn't that what I was doing? Without even knowing what problems might develop, I was already worrying about the bridge.

A friend read the following poem to me:

*I was regretting the past
and fearing the future.
Suddenly my Lord was speaking:
"MY NAME IS 'I AM.'"
I waited. God continued:
"When you live in the past,
with its mistakes and regrets,
it is hard. I am not there.
MY NAME IS NOT 'I WAS.'
"When you live in the future,
with its problems and fears,
it is hard. I am not there.
MY NAME IS NOT 'I WILL BE.'
"When you live in this moment,
it is not hard. I am here.
MY NAME IS 'I AM.'"*[2]

Those words were like a personal reassurance to me from the Lord.

When Nurse Gail came to see Bob the next time, I showed her the poem. I knew she would understand since she was a Christian.

"It's true that God is not the God of the past or the future," she said

[2]Used by permission of Helen Mallicoat.

after she read the poem. "He's the God of the present time—the right now."

She added, "When anyone is in your situation, it's not easy to trust—but isn't that what trust is all about? If we knew all the answers, there wouldn't be any need for trust. Every morning before I go to work, I read about Job and how he trusted God even though he lost his health, his family, and all his possessions."

I was thankful that our hospice nurse was a Christian. Both my needs and Bob's were spiritual as well as physical.

After Nurse Gail left, Bob and I talked more about trust. Even though he felt assured he would be in heaven because of his relationship with Christ, death still loomed as an unknown. Bob's apprehension was understandable.

"It isn't dying that scares me," Bob said. "I know where I am going. It's the mechanics of getting there that bothers me. Will I be in great pain? Will I die gasping for breath?"

Bob's fear of suffocation was real. His type of cancer destroys the bone marrow where red blood cells are made. Red blood cells carry the hemoglobin that supplies oxygen to the body. Already he experienced shortness of breath.

"We have to trust Him for this, too," I said. "Somehow I know that God is going to meet our needs." Saying this bolstered my own faith as much as his. Sometimes my optimism and assurance surprised me as I tried to be strong and encourage Bob.

> *Trust Him when dark doubts assail you,*
> *Trust Him when your strength is small;*
> *Trust Him when to simply trust Him*
> *Seems the hardest thing of all.*[3]

Often I remembered a definition of trust Bob had given years before to a Sunday school class he was teaching: "Trusting God is like standing at the rim of a deep, dark well. God tells you to jump—and you

[3]Bennett, *Our Daily Bread* (July 29, 1994). Used by permission of Radio Bible Class

jump, even though you can't see Him. You take the leap with confidence, knowing that His arms will be there to catch you." It was this kind of trust we both needed now.

As Bob's illness progressed, his mobility became more impaired. He began to experience difficulty in standing and maintaining his balance. One Sunday when I was helping him stand beside the bed to get dressed, he lost his balance and fell forward onto the twin bed in front of him. Sprawled across the mattress, he was completely helpless.

Seconds seemed like hours. Finally he turned to his side, and by using his walker he pulled himself back up. With my support, he returned to his own bed.

The fall didn't hurt him, but it depressed him. He had been in control of his body all of his life. Now he wasn't. The fall robbed him of dignity. It threatened his self-reliance.

"I'm not much use anymore, am I?" he said.

"You sure are to me," I replied, trying to appear lighthearted.

In my search for something—anything—that would help him feel better, I remembered that a friend had told me about a church service on TV every Sunday morning at 10 A.M. This was Sunday morning, just a few minutes past ten o'clock. I turned on the TV. When I flipped to the right channel, the church service was already in progress. The choir was singing:

Because He lives I can face tomorrow,
Because He lives all fear is gone;
Because I know He holds the future.
And life is worth the living just because He lives.

Yes, because He *lives,* my fear is gone! Because He *lives,* I can face the future!

Trust is an anchor that holds us steady in a storm.

Chapter 4

God's Grace PRN

***My grace is sufficient for thee; for my strength is
made perfect in weakness.***
2 CORINTHIANS 12:9

A couple of months before Bob became incapacitated, we were having
lunch in a little restaurant when he said, "You know, we really ought
to make some funeral arrangements."

I had been quietly munching a hot dog with nothing more serious
on my mind than relaxation and people watching. Maybe that's why
his statement startled me so much. Tears clouded my eyes. I couldn't
handle it.

"I didn't want to make you cry," he said, "but maybe we should
think about doing it."

Certainly we both knew the inevitable consequences of his disease—but that day, at that time, I couldn't handle it.

I said, "Some other time."

During my forty years as a nurse, I often gave PRN medications.
That meant the drug or treatment would be given "whenever needed."
During the next few weeks, I discovered God's grace is also given
PRN: whenever needed.

What is grace? I remembered the verse in 2 Corinthians 12:9 where God granted grace to Paul. It empowered him with a strength not his own. In contemplating the future, I prayed that God would give me that kind of grace, too.

Bob's condition deteriorated rapidly after that Easter weekend. His pain became more intense, his breathing more difficult, and his mind more confused. When Bob spoke about funeral arrangements, I had no idea of how soon I would need to deal with them. Would it be weeks—or maybe just days—before they would be needed? Realizing it would be wise to make them ahead of time, I asked our friends, Tom and Bonnie, to stay with Bob for an afternoon while I went to the funeral home. I would have liked Bob with me, but he was too sick.

The sky was overcast, and the parking lot was deserted. The funeral director opened the door and ushered me inside.

"Come upstairs to the office," he said.

We walked past several quiet, dimly lit rooms. Rows of portable straight-backed chairs offered mute testimony to previous funerals. It seemed as if ghosts from the past were in those silent rooms.

His upstairs office, with a large mahogany desk and two swivel chairs in front of it, was familiar. It was the same office where I had made funeral arrangements for my parents. But today was so much different. Today we would be discussing my husband. I remained dry-eyed, and our conversation was calm and professional.

A sealed casket would be placed in a moisture-proof vault in the ground. The director showed me a brochure detailing the attributes of each type of casket and vault according to cost. I chose one of each in a moderate price range.

"Do you want to see the caskets to pick out one?" he asked.

See the caskets? No, thank you. That would come soon enough. Only God's grace kept me from losing my decorum at that point.

"I'll trust your decision," I told him.

He asked me for information for the death certificate and obituary:

Bob's date and place of birth, his parents' names (including his mother's maiden name), and his social security number.

When we finished, I told him to make arrangements for my funeral, too. That way all details would be taken care of so the children would have as little difficulty as possible when the time came for me to die. Saying that wasn't real easy, however; there's nothing like facing your own mortality. But I sailed through it with no problems. God's grace held me together.

That evening I typed out Bob's obituary for our local newspaper. Writing it myself, I could use the phrase "he went home to be with his Lord"—not "he died" or "he passed away." As much as possible, I wanted to honor both Bob and the Lord.

My next hurdle was the cemetery. That seemed like a logical next step. Maybe this was overreacting to my feeling of urgency, but Bob's condition seemed to warrant it.

I phoned the cemetery office early in the morning while Bob was sleeping and made an early appointment. At the cemetery, a surge of memories washed over me. On the left, ducks swam in a quiet pond. Turtles sunned themselves on rocks. When Steve and Gary were young, I often came here with them to feed the ducks and turtles on Sunday afternoons.

Occasionally we would walk back through the cemetery. There were no headstones, just grave markers. Only the outstretched arms of shade trees obscured the horizon, and always an atmosphere of peace prevailed. It seemed natural that this hillside should be our final resting place.

I walked to the edge of the pond. The ducks swam near the shore. My chest felt tight, and my heart ached for happier times. When the escape of tears seemed inevitable, I turned and went to the cemetery office that overlooked the duck pond.

An elderly gentleman greeted me, then reached for a cluster of keys on the wall. "I'll show you the different sites," he said.

"Any site is OK with me," I said. Staring at Bob's actual burial place was a finality I wasn't quite ready to face.

"Time is of the essence," I added. "A friend is staying with my husband."
He nodded. I requested a double lot for Bob and myself.

"Do you want your name engraved on the marker also?" he asked.

"Yes," I replied hesitantly.

"Then your name and the date of your birth will be on the opposite side of the marker from your husband's. The date of death, of course, will be missing." Comforting thought.

A catalog of grave markers offered a limited choice of memorials. I chose a design of interlocking rings. There was a space for the year of our marriage. Having the date of our wedding placed forever on the marker validated our togetherness. It was a comfort to me, as if death was not really going to separate us.

Before leaving the cemetery, I again paused to watch the ducks in the still water. Their world was at peace, filled with sunshine. They were unconcerned that the next day might bring cold, pelting rain with loud claps of thunder and flashes of lightning. Their tranquility was contagious, and I left the cemetery with controlled composure. Once again, God's grace had upheld me.

Writing a family eulogy for the funeral became my next task. I intended to read it myself, so I included details of Bob's conversion to Christ which was the reason for his assurance of heaven. There would be people present who were not Christians, and I wanted to be sure they heard the plan of salvation. I knew Bob would want it that way.

Bob was fifteen years old in Miami, Florida, when he had become convicted of sin in his life. He had never robbed a bank or stolen a car. Probably his worst crime occurred when he was ten years old. While shopping with his mother, he stuffed a pretty new marble in his pocket without paying for it.

It felt right in his fingers—but when he got home and realized what he had done, the marble no longer looked pretty. He felt so convicted of his sin that the next day he went back to the store to return it. He didn't have the courage to face a salesclerk, so he stood just inside the door and rolled the marble down the aisle.

Bob was fifteen when he felt the need to make a personal commit-ment to Jesus. He confessed his unworthiness to the Lord and asked Jesus to forgive him and come into his life. He heard no bells or cym-bals, but he felt the weight lifted from his shoulders. He knew without a doubt he had been forgiven.

The next day he went to his church to talk about it with his pastor and to say he wanted to be baptized. His pastor asked him a question he remembered for the rest of his life: "If you were the only person in the world and Jesus loved you enough to die for you, would you still accept him as your Savior?"

"Yes, I would," Bob said with conviction. He meant it most sin-cerely, and he never strayed from that intent.

I typed the eulogy into my computer the next afternoon. My heart wrote it more than my mind, for I had to do it quickly while Bob took a short nap. Just as I was finishing the last paragraph, he called to me. I saved my work and turned off the computer.

My next project was a collage of pictures. I wanted the casket closed so people would remember Bob as he was in life, not in death. I'm sure Bob would have wanted it this way. Instead of a funeral ser-vice, I decided on a memorial service with pictures showing the high-lights of his life. The funeral-home director loaned me a large, framed board to display photographs.

Bob and I had been married forty-two years and had a wealth of snap-shots and other memorabilia. Selecting pictures was difficult, but finally I chose the ones that best represented his life: a snapshot as a nine-year-old with his arms protruding from the tight sleeves of a too-small jacket; a photo taken in his Navy uniform during World War II; a tinted portrait made when he attended the University of Miami. That's where we met. I took our framed wedding picture out of its holder, and I included spo-radic pictures of our children and grandchildren.The collection included Bob's retirement party from BFGoodrich as well as our last family snapshot from the previous Easter weekend.

I shed a few tears as I reviewed the pictures from our life together.

But God's grace held firm. This gave me added assurance that His grace would *always* be sufficient for me—each and every day, no matter what that day might hold.

His grace also gave me confidence that it would be there for Bob, too, when he needed it. Death is a mystery that none of us truly understands, but we can trust Jesus for His care during our lifetime. And He assures us we can trust Him at the time of our death as well.

In his book *Angels,* Billy Graham wrote that angels will also be present at our passing to help us.[1]

He told the story of a young missionary volunteer who was suddenly taken very ill. She lived only a few hours, and as she died, her young husband and two faculty members from a Bible school were with her. Just before she drew her last breath, she exclaimed, "I see Jesus. I can hear angels singing."[2]

A friend told me that her husband had a similar experience shortly before he died. He had been in a deep coma when suddenly he sat straight up in bed. With his eyes open, he cried, "Hallelujah!"

What did he see? No one knows, but his wife was comforted by what happened. She rushed to his side as he closed his eyes and laid back against the pillows. He died a short time later.

My pastor gave me the following poem entitled *Dying Grace,* written by J. T. Bolding:

When I come to the beautiful end of my day,
And the tides of my life ebb away;
As I'm nearing the finishing line of the race,
Give me, please, O dear Lord, dying grace.

Oh the wonderful prospect of living with Thee!
Oh the joy from all sin to be free!
Oh how great when with Thee we shall have our own place,
And can go there with sweet dying grace.

[1]Billy Graham. *Angels* (Waco, Texas: Word Publishing, 1994), 164.　[2]Ibid., 168.

Until then, grant me Lord, thy good grace just to live,
Day by day as I laugh, love and give;
Then when my time shall come death's cold Jordan to face,
Grant to me, precious Lord, dying grace.

There is "a time to be born, and a time to die" (Ecclesiastes 3:2). When the time came for Bob to go home to his Lord, I felt confident that God's "dying grace" would be there for him.

The prophet Isaiah reminds us that when we call to God, He will answer us (Isaiah 58:9). When we need His grace, whether in life or death, it will be there.

Grace is the glue that can hold a life together.

Chapter 5

Helping Hands and Phone Therapy

Bear ye one another's burdens, and so fulfil the law of Christ.
GALATIANS 6:2

The biweekly visits of Nurse Gail became bright spots in the routine of coping with a progressive illness. She would laugh as she told us about the antics of her teenage son and daughter. We shared the trauma of her son's having his driver's license revoked when he was involved in an accident. We sympathized with her daughter losing her boyfriend when he went to an out-of-town college. We related to her problems, since our kids had generated a few difficulties for us, too. We looked forward to each visit as the next chapter in her continuing saga.

Nurse Gail was a good listener, too. She understood both my emotional and medical problems, and she often had solutions to both. Although I was a nurse, her expertise was different from mine, and I often relied heavily on her knowledge and advice.

During one of her early visits, she noted Bob's increasing confusion when she came into the bedroom and greeted him in her usual cheerful way. "How are things today?" she asked, swinging her heavy black nursing bag onto the opposite twin bed and sitting down.

"Not too good," Bob replied. "I'm having trouble getting out the report for tomorrow's meeting."

Gail squinted a little and glanced at me.

"Bob," she said kindly, "there really isn't any meeting tomorrow. You are a little confused."

Bob considered her statement, then with a puzzled expression said, "They told me there would be a meeting."

"Maybe so," Gail answered, "but I think you might feel better if you had some extra oxygen." She explained to him that his type of cancer often depleted his body's supply of oxygen to his brain.

Gail phoned Bob's oncologist, got an order for oxygen, then called the medical supply company.

"They will bring the oxygen this afternoon," she told us as she prepared to leave, "and I'll check with you tomorrow to see if it helps."

After escorting her to the door, I remarked, "I sure hope he doesn't start seeing bugs in his confusion." Taking care of alcoholics who saw nonexistent bugs crawling over the bedcovers had been part of my nursing experience

Nurse Gail laughed. She had taken care of alcoholics, too. "I don't think you have to worry about bugs."

Later that afternoon a delivery man muscled a heavy green cylindrical oxygen tank into our bedroom. It stood at the end of Bob's bed like a sentry and hissed oxygen through narrow plastic tubing into his nose.

During the night Bob awakened me to help him go to the bathroom. Sleepily I turned on the light and lowered the side rail on his bed. To my surprise, Bob made no attempt to get up.

"Look on the ceiling," he said. "There's a bug up there."

"Now, honey, there is no bug up there," I assured him, taking hold of his hand for consolation.

"What's the matter with you," he snapped. "Can't you see that bug?"

"Bob, you are just confused. There's no bug anywhere."

He insisted he saw a bug. Finally I looked up to the ceiling above his bed. Sure enough, a small, black, long-legged spider was meandering slowly across the ceiling toward the other side of the room.

I laughed. A sense of humor is a necessity when caring for someone who is ill. With a tissue in hand, I balanced myself on the edge of Bob's bed and murdered the intruder.

When Nurse Gail called the next morning, I told her the oxygen was helpful—but maybe he hadn't been as confused as we thought. Then I told her about our nocturnal ceiling bug.

A few days later Nurse Gail ordered an oxygen concentrator to replace the cumbersome cylindrical tank. This machine, about the size of a room humidifier, concentrated room air into pure oxygen. Wheels and tubing made it possible for Bob to walk out to the patio and still receive adequate oxygen. We called the tubing his tether.

The oxygen helped his confusion, but the tubing irritated his nose. When I told Nurse Gail about our new problem, she suggested using a soft pink snap-on curler as a cushion.

By removing the snap-on part, the soft plastic could be fashioned around the tubing to relieve pressure under his nose. Observing my craftsmanship, I remarked, "Your pink mustache makes you look distinguished."

"I don't care what it looks like," Bob said, "as long as it helps my nose." I laughed and called him the Pink Panther.

Bob had other problems, however, and a variety of people helped us with them. Tom and Bonnie scored top place on our helper list. Tom was a retired fireman, and Bonnie didn't work outside the home, so they had the time to offer help. They had time to offer more help than I could have imagined.

Tom and Bonnie thoroughly enjoyed serving God by doing things for people. This made it easy for me to accept their offers to help.

One day I remarked how much I liked to watch the birds. "Would you like a bird feeder?" Tom asked.

"Yes, I would love one," I replied.

"Then we'll get one for you."

A couple of days later he returned with a feeder. He cemented the pole into the ground and added a squirrel baffle under the top part. He procured a birdbath for me as well. He positioned it between two sassafras trees in the backyard and added two large flowerpots filled with red geraniums.

"You've made a regular bird sanctuary," I remarked, as we all admired his handiwork. "Do you think I ought to put a sign up in the yard and charge admission?"

Tom didn't reply. I knew he had a hearing problem, but lately it had worsened to where lipreading was almost mandatory. Bonnie gently nudged him to let him know I had said something. When he looked back to me, I repeated my exclamation.

"I'm glad you like it," he said proudly.

Bonnie, too, gave generously of herself. When Bob was still able to come to the table to eat, more than once she cooked dinner at home and brought it to our house, and she and Tom joined us for the meal. We enjoyed the food, but of more importance to us was their fellowship.

Bonnie's greatest help was her phone calls. Each evening she called to ask how my day had gone. Unlike some of my other friends, she didn't tell me *her* problems. She let me tell her mine. She let me unload, and I looked forward each evening to her call. As Bob's illness progressed, I often felt isolated, as if the four walls were closing in on me, and she became my contact with the outside world.

I am sure that calling me was an inconvenience at times, but no matter where she was, she phoned me. As Bob's condition worsened, just that contact with another human was the lifeline I needed to keep my sanity.

Toward the end of Bob's illness, she often called in the afternoon, too. "Just making a sanity check," she would say when I picked up the phone. Then she would chat for just a few minutes.

Other friends and neighbors also helped. One night after Bob had gone to sleep and the quiet house was making me feel exceptionally lonely, a friend called to ask if I would like to have a freshly baked cake. A freshly baked cake? At ten in the evening?

When I expressed surprise, she said, "I had a 'starter cake' that had to be baked tonight after I got home from work, and I thought you might like to have it. Is it OK if I bring it over?"

"Sure," I said, grateful that I would have contact with another living soul. "But what is a starter cake?"

She laughed, then explained it was made with batter that must be used within a certain time frame or it would spoil. It involved a regimen of adding specified ingredients on certain days till the tenth day when half the batter was baked. The other half went into the refrigerator to start the procedure all over again.

A few minutes later, Barbara presented me with a loaf cake wrapped in foil. I thanked her profusely. She had eased my loneliness with her friendship, relieving my tension like a soothing cup of tea at the end of a busy day.

The still-warm cake was delicious, but her concern, her expression of love, meant more to me than the chocolate treat. As I nibbled the cake, accompanied by a glass of milk, my problems didn't seem quite so oppressive.

Several other people also helped us in a variety of other ways.

Bob's problem with constipation had become a major concern. The more the doctor increased his narcotics, the worse it became. Regulating his laxatives was a challenge.

One day Bob had an acute need for the bathroom. Immediately I tried to help him out of bed, but the urgency of the moment became too much for him. His foot slipped, and he slumped down between the bed and the nightstand.

Bob was too weak to get himself up, and he was too heavy for me to lift. I had no idea how he was going to get back to bed, let alone to the bathroom.

My neighbor was mowing his lawn, so I ran outside and frantically hailed him. He helped lift Bob to his feet, then got him to the adjacent bathroom. We were thankful for his help, but both Bob and I were a little embarrassed by this necessary invasion of our privacy.

When my composure returned, I remembered the verse of scripture that says that "before they call, I will answer" (Isaiah 65:24). It was then that I *really* thanked God, for just minutes before our need was apparent, He had supplied a neighbor willing to help.

A different kind of help came from our family. At the end of May, Gary and Dana spent a weekend with us to plant flowers and add landscaping. Dana loved flowers, and Gary supplied much of the work.

In previous years I had planted a few petunias along the front of the house, but that was the extent of my gardening. Dana and Gary put in alyssum, verbena, salvia, columbine, and coleus. By the hedge in the backyard, Gary also created a miniature rock garden where he planted a snowball tree and begonias. Never before did I have such exotic gardens.

As Bob and I sat on the patio watching them, he asked, "Do you think Gary will marry Dana?"

"I hope so," I replied. "What do you think?"

"My vote is no. Gary is married to an airplane."

I often thought the same thing. Gary had always loved planes and being a pilot. All he ever wanted to do in life was fly. When he went to college, he knew his major would have something to do with flying. He never wavered from that ambition. In high school and college, he had dated infrequently. Flying consumed his entire focus. Dana, in fact, was his first serious girlfriend.

We enjoyed the weekend. As Dana and Gary were preparing to leave, Bob asked me for paper and a pencil. When I handed it to him, he pulled the bedside table across his legs and pushed the lever to raise up his head on the pillow. Quickly he wrote a note, then handed it to Dana.

"Don't read it till you're in the car," he told her.

Later I learned what he had written: "To Dana—I do not know how long God has given me, but I can't consider any better choice for my son's life than you. When you have seen this, then show it to Gary and Mom. Sincerely, Dad-Bob."

Bob, who seldom showed emotion, had opened up a facet of his life that I had never seen before.

As summer wore on, friends' notes and cards meant a great deal to us, especially to Bob. He looked forward to the mail each day. Cards were his contact with the outside world, and his assurance that others cared.

I particularly appreciated the cards that were addressed to both of us. This let me know that others realized I was having a difficult time, too. When they wrote our names at the top of the greeting section or underlined some of the words in the verse for emphasis, I felt this was a personal message and not just a commercial remembrance. A short sentence like "I'm praying for you" gave me a spiritual lift. When you're hurting, little things mean a lot.

Before Bob became ill, I was never quite certain how to give comfort to others or offer help. Experience is the crucible in which lessons are learned, however, and I now know exactly how to do it. If there is a need, fill it. If a garden needs weeding, pull the weeds. If a friend is hungry, bring a meal. If shut-ins are lonely, visit them.

One word sums it up: love. Without the show of God's love, nothing else matters much (see 1 Corinthians 13:13).

A helping hand is a handy help.

Chapter 6

A Rocky Roller Coaster

[Jesus said], "My peace I give unto you. . . .
Let not your heart be troubled."
JOHN 14:27

During Bob's illness my emotions resembled a roller coaster. Just as little cars chug up a track to great heights, then swoop down with lightning speed, my feelings changed with similar swiftness and variance.

Tears were often near the surface as I experienced loneliness, helplessness, frustration, boredom—and guilt. Coping was not easy.

As Bob's illness progressed, boredom was the hardest to deal with. There was no escaping its pressure. Bob wasn't able to be left alone, so hour after hour, day after day, I was confined to the house.

Gail listed three reasons why it was dangerous to leave Bob alone: Could he call on a phone if he needed help? Could he get out of the house if there was a fire? Was he mentally alert enough to perceive danger? As Bob's clear thinking and ability to move decreased, the risk in his being alone increased. The possibility of his falling and getting seriously hurt was very real. I couldn't go anywhere or do anything.

Before Bob became acutely ill, I had gone to a senior-citizen aerobics class three mornings a week. Once a month I met friends for lunch. An assortment of church activities kept me busy. Bob and I usually went to church twice on Sundays and to Bible study and prayer meeting on Wednesday evenings. All of this was put on hold, and all days ground down to a monotonous routine.

My role changed from wife to caregiver. Frustration wore me down as I tried to inject meaning into my days. I tried to interest Bob in television, but he wasn't able to comprehend what was happening. He even lost interest in the Cleveland Indians and in the Browns football games. Before his illness he rarely missed a televised game.

In the hope of reviving his interest, I had a sports channel added to our TV. All that accomplished, however, was more confusion. The added channel meant he had one more remote control to negotiate—and he couldn't handle it.

Friends loaned us videos, but he couldn't understand the movie plots and usually asked to have them turned off. I tried to interest him in our local Christian radio station, but after a few minutes, he would shut it off.

Normal conversation was nearly out of the question. I could read some, but even that was frustrated by his frequent interruptions.

I always enjoyed using my computer in the basement, but after just a few minutes apart from Bob, he would call me. Usually his voice had a frantic tone to it. I would race up the stairs, expecting to find some emergency, and he would merely want to know how long before lunch. I soon gave up trying to do anything on the computer. Boredom reigned supreme.

"Please, God," I prayed often, "help me to be understanding. Help me to have *Your* patience and *Your* joy."

There were days when I felt as if the house was my prison. Watching my neighbors come and go made me wish I was free to do the same. Sometimes I would feel resentful. Then I would feel guilty, for there was only one way I would ever again be free to do what I wanted.

I would pray to be forgiven for my thoughts. Then I would remind myself that Philippians 4:6 tells me to be anxious for nothing—but in *everything* to bring my problems to Him with thanksgiving. Thanksgiving?

Being thankful was difficult till I remembered my blessings: ordinary things such as a comfortable home, adequate food, and my own good health that allowed me to hear and see and move about. I was also thankful for the strength that allowed me to keep Bob at home, and when I remembered the blessing of having him still with me, each day became a precious gift.

I was thankful, too, that I could bring my burdens to the Lord and leave them there. When my problems seemed to close in on me, I would often remember a tract that said, "Lord, for *this* I have You." And I was glad I could rely on Him to say, "For *this* You have Me."

I was reminded of the poem titled *Footprints,* which was one of Bob's favorites. He referred to it often as the days became heavy. Its message was reassuring: "Lord, You said that once I decided to follow You, You'd walk with me all the way. But I have noticed that during the most troublesome times in my life, there is only one set of footprints. I don't understand why, when I needed You most, You would leave me."

Then the Lord replies, "My precious, precious child, I love you and I would never leave you during your times of trial and suffering. When you saw only one set of footprints, it was then that I carried you."

Besides boredom, other forms of stress became a part of my life. One day Bob decided to clean out the top drawer in the nightstand next to his bed. It held a variety of outlines from Bible studies he had once taught, as well as accumulated pamphlets and other memorabilia. Acknowledging that it was something to keep him busy for a while, I willingly accommodated him by getting the wastebasket.

Bob had always had a habit of tearing into shreds anything he was going to discard. While I did a few things in the kitchen, he spent the next hour happily ripping paper into tiny bits. Afterward I discovered he had destroyed the instruction booklets to the snowblower, the lawn mower, and the clock radio.

Once again, I gave the problem to Jesus. It didn't change the situation, but it helped my attitude.

In spite of Bob's presence, I was often very lonely. As Bob's mental condition deteriorated, he was not much companionship. I longed for interaction with another human being. Friends from church did stop by to see us, but there were hours when I was alone—and lonely.

One day while Bob was napping, I went outside to pull a few weeds in the flowers underneath his bedroom window. Hearing him would be no problem if he needed me. With my hands in the flower bed, I saw a UPS truck stop at the curb. The delivery man hopped out and took a package next door. I had the strongest urge to run over and ask if he would talk to me. Just a friendly hello would be helpful.

Then laughing at myself, I said half aloud, "Things are really pretty bad when you're so lonely you want to disrupt the schedule of the UPS man just so you can talk to someone."

I had to remind myself: for *this* I have Jesus.

Again guilt became a factor. In early June when Bob was able to go outside to the patio extension, I did a little gardening. I planted pachysandra along the back fence and begonias by the hedge in one corner of the yard. Later that night I felt guilty because I hadn't spent the time with Bob. I realized our time together was short—was planting flowers really that important?

Yet what could I have done with him except just sit beside him? Guilt told me maybe that's what should have been done. The one line of poetry I remembered from my high school English class was found in Milton's "Sonnet on His Blindness:" "They also serve who only stand and wait." Sometimes the most important thing we can do is to "do nothing."

I also felt guilty for being healthy when Bob was sick, as if somehow I ought to be able to share the disability with him and lessen his suffering. This guilt had no substance to it, but still it haunted me.

At the end of each day, turning over my problems to the Lord made me feel better. For *this* I had Jesus.

One morning I stubbed my toe when getting the newspaper from the front porch after a rather sleepless night. I cried out under my breath, "Will this ever end?!!" Guilt washed over me. Only one way was it going to end, and I felt humiliated for wanting the release.

At times I was bone tired. Bob would awaken me two or three times during the night. He would rattle the side rails on his bed, and I dreaded hearing that noise. Guilt prodded me if I didn't get up right away.

My patience and strength seemed stretched to the breaking point at times. Bob didn't intend to be demanding, but often he let his needs become his primary focus. When we were still able to eat our meals together in the dining room, as soon as he was finished, he wanted me to help him back to bed, whether I was through with my meal or not. His pain was worse when sitting up, and he wanted to lie down. Usually I left my food half-eaten and never got back to it. There was a fringe benefit to this, however: losing the ten pounds I had been trying to trim off for five years.

As Bob's illness progressed, our early morning routine became even more taxing. As soon as he was awake, he wanted his pain pills, the bed straightened, the newspaper from the front porch, and his breakfast. Never mind if I had time to get dressed or not.

To help keep my sanity, I mentally devised a contest to see how many tasks could be accomplished before he reminded me what should be done next. Silently I would give myself a test score. By doing this, his requests became a challenge rather than an irritation.

At times, the feeling of helplessness was almost overpowering. There was so little I could do for Bob. I tried to prepare appealing meals, but his waning appetite made him want very little to eat. He continually lost weight. When I encouraged him to come out to the patio and enjoy the afternoon sunshine, he complained about the heat and soon wanted to return to the air-conditioned bedroom. We tried playing checkers, but he couldn't remember which color he was playing with or in which direction he was going.

Once again, for *this* I had Jesus.

Bob, too, had his areas of frustration. It hurt him to have other people, including me, doing chores he was used to doing. I knew he felt humiliated when he had to sit idly in a chair with his oxygen while our neighbor climbed onto our patio roof to scoop out the gutters clogged with spring blossoms from an overhanging tree. This had always been Bob's yearly task.

We were forced to use a lawn service to cut the grass Bob had always mowed. Even my taking the trash to the curb each week reminded him that he could no longer do it.

And the specter of death was always with him. One day as he maneuvered his walker down the back step to the patio while I held onto his belt to steady him, he said simply, "I know I have to die." He didn't look at me when he said it. He spoke quietly, as if making just a simple declaration, but it told me the prospect of death was ever present in his mind. It was the assurance of heaven that was a comfort to both of us.

For *all* this, we both had Jesus.

The one thing I *could* do for Bob was to assure him of my love—no matter what the circumstances. Sharing a hug became a vital link to life for us. I would put down the side rail of his bed, lean across his chest and embrace him. He would envelop me with his arms, and we would give each other a mutual squeeze. Afterward I would rest my head on his chest for a few seconds. The rhythmic beating of his heart would comfort me and strengthen our bond of love. We called this togetherness our "hug time."

One day as I sat on the edge of his bed, Bob cupped my face in his hands and looked a long time into my eyes. Finally he said, "You are so beautiful. And I love you so much."

Being far from beautiful, I was thankful that "beauty is in the eyes of the beholder." His opinion was all that mattered to me.

Tears came to my eyes. "I love you, too," I said.

Love is listed first in the category of spiritual fruit. Perhaps it is a better reflection of Christ in our life than any other attribute.

To lighten the load, share the weight with God.

The Marathon Race

Let us lay aside every weight, and the sin which doth so
easily beset us, and let us run with patience the
race that is set before us.

HEBREWS 12:1

Toward the end of July when Bob was maneuvering his walker from the bedroom to the adjacent bathroom, he said, "There's something I want to ask you." Even though it was nine o'clock in the morning, his tone was very serious.

"OK, what is it?"

He looked away, his voice quivered a little, and he asked, "Would you think ill of me if I took my own life?"

The question jolted me. Did I hear him correctly?

"What did you say?"

He repeated the question in a monotone. "Would you think ill of me if I took my own life?"

I knew he was tired of being sick, and I knew there was little joy in having only death to look forward to, but to know Bob was contemplating suicide was startling. I waited a few seconds before answering, wanting to be sure of saying the right thing.

"No, I wouldn't think ill of you. I would still love you—very much—but I sure hope you don't do it."

"Do you think I would lose my salvation?"

"No, but you might lose your Christian witness. Think of your sons and grandchildren."

If they found out he had taken his own life, would they think he was a coward? Would that be the one thing they would remember most about him—crowding out their memory of his love for them, the gifts he had given them, and the Christian testimony he had tried to live before them?

"Don't worry," he said. "I don't have the guts to kill myself."

"I'm glad of that," I replied, trying to respond in a lighthearted manner. "I would really like to keep you around."

Reaching for his hand, and looking into his eyes, I said in almost a whisper, "I know it's tough. But when things get tough, that's when God gives us *His* courage."

Courage? I remembered the courage Bob displayed when he forced himself to go back to work after his first bout with cancer. Never in his life had he been a quitter. Never had he run from a challenge.

The temptation to quit was strong, but God's Word assures us of divine help in our greatest need: "God is faithful; he will not let you be tempted beyond what you can bear. But when you are tempted [tested], he will provide a way out so that you can stand up under it" (1 Corinthians 10:13, NIV).

I thanked God that He helped me recall His Word at those times when I needed it the most. Yes, God would provide "a way out." He had done it in the past; He would do it in the future. Our responsibility was just to trust Him that His grace would be there.

Neither Bob nor I said anything more about his question, and I thought the matter was settled. That afternoon, however, it surfaced again during our pastor's visit.

Bob and I were sitting outside on the patio extension when Pastor Davies came. We greeted him and invited him to join us. Summer sunshine warmed the backyard, and we welcomed the shade of the overhanging patio roof. As we watched a couple of squirrels chasing each other around the bird feeder, we chatted about happenings at church.

There was a pause in the conversation. Bob said, "Pastor, I want to ask you a question. Would you think ill of me if I took my own life?"

If the pastor was as surprised as I had been, he didn't show it. He thought for a long moment before replying.

"You know, Bob," he said, "life is like a marathon race. If you quit running in the twenty-sixth mile and never reach the finish line, people will never remember that you ran at all. It only matters if you finish the race. And you are in that twenty-sixth mile.

"Over the years you have been a witness for our Lord to many people. You've taught Sunday school. You've been a Bible study leader. Do you know that many people at church admire you today for the courage you have shown in the face of cancer?"

"It isn't easy," Bob said quietly.

"No one ever said it was easy," Pastor added, "but you have done it. And with our Lord's help, you can continue to do it."

Pastor Davies opened his Bible to the eighth chapter of Romans. "God's Word assures us that in all things we can be conquerors through Him Who loves us. And nothing—not even death—can separate us from the love of God, which is in Christ Jesus our Lord."

"I know that," Bob said softly.

"God is sovereign," Pastor said. "He never makes a mistake. Often His timetable for life and death isn't the same as ours (see Isaiah 55:9), but His timing is perfect. And we have no right to trample on His will."

Pastor closed his Bible. "Shall we pray?"

The three of us went together before the throne of God while Pastor Davies brought our needs before the Almighty. When he finished praying, Bob thanked him for his help.

Before Pastor Davies left, he paused by Bob's chair and placed a hand on his shoulder. "How do you want me to continue praying for you?" he asked.

Without a moment's hesitation, Bob replied, "Pray that I will remain faithful to the end. And that I will be an example to others for Christ."

In any race, the twenty-sixth mile is always the most difficult. That's when God gives us our "second wind." We look to Jesus, the "author and finisher of our faith" (Hebrews 12:2), to help us run that final mile, cross the finish line, and triumphantly declare, "I have fought the good fight, I have finished the race, I have kept the faith" (2 Timothy 4:7, NIV).

To win the race, watch the Lord.

Chapter 8

Rocks, Pots, and Photographs

Give, and it shall be given unto you; good measure,
pressed down, and shaken together, and running over.
Luke 6:38

Flat rocks and squares of cement formed a walkway in front of the pachysandra along the basement wall near our patio. Over the years, moss and grass had overtaken their borders. They needed a cleanup job.

During one of Gary's weekend visits, I pointed out my latest concern. "Those rocks are a mess," I said. "I should take them out and let the grass grow instead."

"Do you want me to do it?" he asked.

"Yes," I replied. "I would appreciate it."

Before he went back to Columbus, Gary loosened the rocks and cement squares with a shovel and piled them up beside the patio.

A few days later when I went outside, I noticed gaping holes in the ground where the rocks and slabs had been. New dirt would be needed before grass could be planted. Where would I get any dirt? Maybe digging them up hadn't been such a good idea after all.

I decided the best solution was to clean off the slabs and put them

49

back where they had been. After lunch I persuaded Bob to sit in the shade on the patio and watch me work.

I got him settled with his oxygen in a chair by the picnic table, then asked him if he wanted to read a book or listen to the radio.

"No, I will just watch you work."

I got a scrub brush and a bucket with water. I scrubbed at the moss and tried to rinse off the resulting mud with water from the bucket. Then Bob had a suggestion. "If you'd use the garden hose, it would be easier."

Why didn't I think of that? I hooked up the hose and used a forceful spray to clean off the slabs. It worked much better than my bucket approach.

Then Bob had another suggestion. "Give me the hose and I'll wash the slabs off after you scrub them."

I wasn't sure this was feasible, but Bob insisted. I realized just sitting and watching me work was hard on his ego and self-esteem. Feeling needed was important to him.

Bob told me exactly how to position the slabs near his chair so he could squirt them with the hose one at a time. I moved several of them closer to him, then proceeded to scratch off moss from the rest of them. As Bob executed his part of the project, I paid little attention to what he was doing.

When I looked back at him, I found he had not only washed the cement slabs, he had washed himself. Mud had splattered all over him, the picnic table, and the patio. His slippers were soaked.

"Bob!" I said loudly. "Look what you're doing!"

He was oblivious to the mess, looking at me with a blank, childlike innocent expression.

"You're soaking wet," I declared, my tone angry.

Taking him back inside the house seemed to be the only solution. I shut off the water and helped him go inside with his walker. He had an early sponge bath that day. When Nurse Gail came later that afternoon, I explained to her why he was in his pajamas instead of being dressed.

Self-esteem has a price, I guess.

A few days later, we had another crisis. The toilet overflowed, and I dashed to the basement for the plunger while Bob grabbed a towel to soak up the water.

By the time I got back upstairs, an inch of water had flooded the bathroom floor. The plunger took care of the flushing problem, but we were left with the flood.

"Let me get you back to bed," I said, "and I'll get things cleaned up."

Bob ignored my suggestion. "Give me another towel," he muttered as he wrung out the first towel. "I'm OK."

Helping me was important to him. When he insisted on helping, I conceded.

By the time all was dry, Bob's breathing was heavy, and his color was pasty. Even the following day found him fatigued. I told Nurse Gail what had happened.

"He used up all his oxygen reserve. It will take him at least two or three days to recover."

She was right. Once again self-esteem showed its cost.

The following Friday, Gary flew home for an unexpected visit. Gary found a ride home from the airport, but the return trip was up to me. When he asked me if I could handle that, I said, "Sure, I can find someone to stay with Daddy while I take you to the airport."

As usual, the someone I had in mind was Tom and Bonnie. However, they volunteered to take Gary back themselves.

"Besides, I would like to see the plane," Tom said.

Gary showed him the cockpit and explained the instruments to him. Bonnie told me afterward that they had had a good time. A few weeks later they asked if they could stop by after church. "We have something we want to give you. It's a surprise."

Bob and I speculated what their surprise might be. They presented us with a framed picture of Gary in the cockpit of his company's plane. Tom had taken the picture when they had taken Gary back to the airport.

Tom held the picture up against the wall so we could see what it would look like when it was hanging.

"That is one of the best pictures of Gary I have ever seen," I said. "It was so nice of you to do that."

When Tom didn't reply, Bonnie realized he hadn't heard me and told him I had been speaking to him. I repeated what I had just said.

"I'm glad you like it," Tom said. "We had fun doing it."

After they left, Bob and I talked about Tom's hearing problem. Tom felt his stint of nearly twenty-five years as a firefighter working around blaring sirens had probably caused his deafness, but workman's compensation refused to acknowledge this or pay for a hearing aid. Hearing aids are expensive, and Tom's limited pension didn't allow the extravagance of purchasing one.

"Do you think we could afford to get a hearing aid for Tom?" Bob asked.

Since I am the family treasurer, I thought a moment about our financial status. "I think we could," I replied. In addition to our pensions and social security, we had a small inheritance from my parents.

Bob's next question wasn't as easily answered. "Do you think Tom will let us do it?"

"I don't know. We can try."

We both knew Tom to be a proud person. No way did we want to offend him by drawing attention to his disability or making him feel he was accepting charity. For a Christian, giving is often easier that receiving.

I remembered an incident many years before when Liz Boyer, my best friend, took me to see a Shakespearean play. We were both recently married and neither of us had much money. When I protested at her extravagance, she replied, "Now don't be ungracious. I want to do it."

No one wants to be considered ungracious. I have always remembered that.

When Pastor Davies visited us the next time, we broached the problem with him.

"We'd like to get a hearing aid for Tom," Bob said, "not because he's done so much for us but because we just want to do it. It would mean a lot to me if he would let us buy it for him."

"If you put it to him that way, I don't see how he can refuse," Pastor replied.

The next time Tom and Bonnie came to see us, Bob told him our intention. Tom looked abashed but delighted. When he finally found words to speak, he said, "Nobody has ever done anything that nice for me before."

"Then it's about time there was a change," Bob retorted.

After a few medical tests and several fittings for the right-sized hearing aid, Tom came to us one day and proudly demonstrated his new hearing ability. I saw a look of joy in Bob's face that hadn't been there for a long time.

A few days later a thank-you card came from Bonnie. On it she wrote the following note: "Bob, you are a very special channel that God used to answer my prayer. I have been praying for a way to help Tom's hearing problem, and you became 'that way.' As Tom enjoys each new sound, he and I will be reminded of you and your continuing faithful service to the Lord—even on your sickbed!"

There is no better remedy for low self-esteem than the satisfaction of a giving heart.

Giving gives more joy than getting.

Chapter 9

Special Days and Tough Tenderness

This is the day which the Lord hath made;
we will rejoice and be glad in it.

Psalm 118:24

Time becomes precious when there is little of it left, and holidays become difficult as everyone realizes these are probably the last ones they will celebrate with their loved one.

Mother's Day was our first holiday after Bob's illness became acute. Ever since our children were born, he has remembered that special day with a card and a small gift.

One year, though, he nearly forgot. "Oh my!" he exclaimed. "I forgot. Tomorrow is Mother's Day. I haven't gotten anything for you yet."

"That's all right," I said. "I know you love me. That's what counts."

Rain was pouring down. Wind and lightning would make driving difficult.

"No, it isn't all right. I'm going to the store right now."

"In this storm!?" I cried. "For goodness sake, don't go to the store now."

He was not deterred. He drove through the storm to the shopping center. When he returned, he was triumphantly carrying his purchase. He had accomplished his mission.

The next morning when I opened the little box, I found a heart-shaped crystal on a golden chain. Inexpensive—but a priceless gift I have always treasured.

I knew he would feel bad this year since he couldn't get out to buy a gift. I wished that somehow we could bypass the day without his knowing it had occurred. But that wouldn't happen. A few days before Mother's Day, I discovered a white envelope tucked under the cover of a book on the TV stand. I thought it might be a card. I didn't know how it got there, but I was quite certain I knew what it was.

On Mother's Day, after we had eaten breakfast, Bob said to me, "There is something I want you to get for me."

"What is it?"

"Look inside the top book on the TV stand."

I pretended to fumble with the books; then I picked up the one in which I had seen the envelope and asked if this was the book he wanted.

"That's the one," he said. "Now look inside it."

I raised the cover of the book and showed great surprise when I found it concealed a white envelope. As I opened it, Bob said, "I couldn't let Mother's Day go by without giving you a card. I asked Gary to buy it for me when he was home the last time."

As I read the card, tears came to my eyes; I will keep it forever.

Father's Day had a different perspective. It was my turn to give—mine and the boys. Gary made certain that he could come home for Father's Day. After Sunday dinner, we presented Bob with his gifts. In addition to a card, I gave him a large plastic container of gum-drops, his favorite candy. Gary gave him a card and a candle in the shape of a train locomotive.

A candle might seem like a strange Father's Day gift, but Gary knew his father liked trains. Toy trains had always fascinated him, and he became a little boy again around train memorabilia.

Gary had purchased the candle for his dad's birthday in late August. Because Bob's condition had continually worsened and we felt he might not be with us for his birthday, Gary decided to give him the candle on Father's Day instead.

Gary also gave his father a little book titled *To a Very Special Dad.* Inside on the flyleaf, he wrote, "To my father, who is very special to me and whom I love very much. Your son, Gary."

Gary had difficulty expressing love. He was two years younger than his brother. He had lived in his brother's shadow and as a result, put up a barricade around himself that was not easily penetrated. His dad's illness opened up a wellspring of emotion in him.

Before Gary went to bed, he asked me to read the book to his dad. The book said things he had never been able to say. This was his way of making sure his dad heard them now. He was afraid Bob might not read it himself.

I got Bob ready for the night; then I sat beside his bed. The book listed the attributes of a father. One section was titled "Memories of Happy Days." It was a show of gratitude from a son, thanking his dad for the many things he had done for him.

Steve called his dad on Father's Day, but he waited until the following weekend to give him a gift. On a business trip, he arranged for a stopover in Ohio on his way back to California.

My husband had been in the navy and still had an affection for ships. Steve's gift was a tiny glass clipper ship encased in a small bottle. The bottle was about six inches long and rested on a wooden pedestal. We dubbed it "the boat in a bottle."

The hours Steve spent with us that weekend were precious, and we tried to crowd into them everything that needed to be said. We all knew this was undoubtedly the last time Steve would see his dad.

After dinner Steve had to leave. The parting was tearful. He hugged his dad and said, "I love you so much"; then he turned and left quickly.

Last times together are difficult—but how wonderful to have the assurance that we will all be together again in heaven someday.

Each day is a twenty-four-hour gem given by God.

Chapter 10

Leave a Legacy

I thank my God upon every remembrance of you.
PHILIPPIANS 1:3

Love is a special commodity, especially the love for children or grand-children. One afternoon when time hung heavy for us, Bob expressed regret that he would have to leave his grandchildren.

"I'll never see Zak play baseball again," he said. "I'll never see him go to high school or college. I won't be there when he gets his license to drive or when he does any of those things a teenage boy does. I won't see Gwen when she has her first date or when she gets married."

Then came the hardest realization of all. "And Kit. Kit probably won't even remember me." Kit was two years old.

I searched for words of encouragement. "Kit will know you by what others tell her about you. And she will have pictures of you."

"But she won't *know* me."

Recalling the note he had written to Dana, I suggested he also write a note to each of the grandchildren: a personal letter from their grandfather, a legacy they could treasure when they were much older.

"What could I say to them?" he asked.

"Just write something you would like them to know about you," I said, "or something you want them to remember."

Bob never put a high price on anything emotional, so I pursued the idea over the next couple of days. Finally he agreed to write each of them a note.

I carefully chose notepaper that I thought would be appropriate for each child: a wreath of roses for four-year-old Gwen. She was always the "little lady" and enjoyed wearing pretty dresses and frilly socks.

For nine-year-old Zak, I found notepaper with the picture of a little boy wielding a shovel of dirt to help his sister plant a tree. And for Kit—what else but a picture of a fluffy, gray kitten with his head cocked to one side.

I positioned the bedside table across Bob's knees and gave him his favorite pen.

"What shall I write?" he asked.

"Write any message you want them to have."

Bob considered that prospect for a few minutes, then started to write. I watched as his unsteady hand printed letters that formed an uneven line. What he wrote made no sense as his brain gave scrambled messages to his pen. Words were misspelled. Even the date was scratched over several times. But he signed each card with clear strokes: Gampi. The children always called him Gampi. I was Mimi, and he was Gampi.

That evening when I saw how tired he was, I realized such a project had not been a good idea. I was uncertain whether or not I should send the cards to Steve. Did I want something illegible to be a legacy for the children?

I asked Steve about it one evening when he phoned. I told him about the note-writing fiasco.

"Maybe he could talk to the kids on a cassette tape," Steve suggested.

That sounded like a good idea to me, although Bob didn't think too highly of that idea either.

Finally, I hit on an alternate suggestion. "How about recording the "Hawaiian Wedding Song" you used to sing when the kids were little?"

When Bob was in the navy and spent some time in Honolulu, he learned a song in the Hawaiian native tongue. It had the rhythmic sound of a hula dance, and when he sang it, I could always picture a dark-haired young lady in a grass skirt swaying to the tune. As Steve and Gary were growing up, Bob had entertained them many times by singing his Hawaiian chant for them. They always responded with good-natured giggles.

The year before Bob became incapacitated, he and I had taken a tour of Hawaii. The trip included a boat ride to a grotto on Kauai. There was a young Hawaiian lady singing the same song Bob had so often sung. She called it the "Hawaiian Wedding Song," but the words sounded the same as those Bob had intoned over the years. Bob didn't know what the words meant in English, but he knew how to sing them in the Hawaiian dialect.

I prepared the cassette recorder with a new tape, and a couple of afternoons later we used our bedroom as a recording studio. After I pushed the button to record, Bob sang a few words of the song, then stopped.

"That's not right," he said. "I'll have to start over."

I rewound the tape, and we started over. Once again he faltered after just a few bars of the song. He used to rattle through it with no difficulty.

"I need something to sing to," Bob said finally. Looking around for something he could serenade, he spotted the boat in the bottle that Steve had given him for Father's Day.

"Let me sing to the boat," he said. I gave it to him. As he held it up in front of him and concentrated on the tiny sails inside their glass casing, he sang the words perfectly to his "Hawaiian Wedding Song." I heaved a sigh of relief when he finished.

A few days later a young man from our church offered a different kind of legacy. Jeff Brown had been in the primary-age Sunday school class Bob had taught. Bob often laughed about the year Christmas fell on a Sunday. In the middle of the lesson, he looked over to Jeff and found him sound asleep with his head propped up against his hand. Obviously he had gotten up early to find the gifts Santa had left, and fatigue had overtaken him.

Jeff was now a young man in his early thirties and married to a vivacious girl named Jamie. It was a Sunday afternoon when Jeff and Jamie came by to see us.

For almost an hour we discussed Jeff's photography business and talked about what had been happening at church. When it was time for them to leave, Jeff handed Bob a scroll rolled up like a diploma and tied with a ribbon.

"This is for you," Jeff told him.

Bob unfurled the scroll and read what was printed on it. The words were from a song titled "Thank You."[1]

I dreamed I went to heaven
and you were there with me.
We walked along the streets of gold
beside the crystal sea.
We heard the angels singing,
then someone called your name.
You turned and saw a young man,
and he was smiling as he came.
He said, "Friend, you may not know me now,"
and then he said, "but wait.
You used to teach my Sunday school
when I was only eight.
And every week you said a prayer
before the class would start.
One day when you said that prayer

I asked Jesus in my heart!
So thank you, for giving to the Lord
For I am a life that was changed!
Thank you for giving to the Lord
I am so glad you gave!"

Below the poem, written in the same script, were these words:

As a result of your diligent ministry to the youth of our church, I had the wonderful privilege of accepting Jesus as my personal Savior when I was only eight years old. I sang this song a few months ago in the morning worship service and silently dedicated it to you. God bless you!
    In Christian love and gratitude,
    Jeff and Jamie Brown.

Tears glistened in Bob's eyes. There is no greater reward than knowing that God has used you to bring another soul to the Savior.

I had the scroll mounted and framed. I put it on the dresser as a constant reminder to Bob that his life had indeed been one in which he had served his Lord—a crown to someday place at the feet of Jesus.

A life remembered is a lasting legacy.

Chapter 11

A Heavenly Supply Line

Thus saith the Lord . . . : "Call unto me, and I will answer thee."
JEREMIAH 33:2-3

Prayer is a two-way conversation with our Lord. We tell Him our praise and problems; then He speaks to us in our heart and through His Word—and takes care of our needs.

One of my greatest difficulties during Bob's illness was his need for constant attention. Regardless of where I went, in a short time he would be calling my name. If I didn't respond right away, his yell became louder. He seldom wanted anything more than to know where I was. I felt as if I was on an invisible tether. But God had an answer to my problem—one I would never have thought of myself.

The solution to my invisible tether difficulty came during Steve's Father's Day weekend visit. After dinner the first evening he was home, he and I went outside while I showed him the pachysandra I had planted in front of the hedge. We were there only a few seconds when Bob yelled for me.

I groaned a little. "This being constantly on call is so frustrating," I remarked as I left to go back inside the house.

Afterward Steve said to me, "I know something that might help. What you need is our baby monitor."

Baby monitor? Steve explained that when Kit was a baby, they had placed a monitor by her at night so they would know if she had any problems. If she whimpered or cried, they heard her. They couldn't talk to her, but the monitor would alert them to her need. It could work the same way now for Bob.

Steve sent me the monitor when he got back home. Powered by small batteries, one gizmo could sit like a silent sentry on the dresser by Bob's bed, and I could carry the other one outside, attached to a pocket or my waistband. The range wasn't great, but it was enough to allow me to go to the backyard or the basement. I could hear every breath Bob took, and knowing that all he had to do was speak and I would hear him, he no longer needed to yell.

A similar problem was solved by the car telephone. A few weeks before Bob became incapacitated, we purchased a mobile phone. I wanted it for safety in case of an accident, flat tire, or other emergency.

Every Thursday morning, a nurse's aide provided by hospice came to stay with Bob for three or four hours while I did all the week's errands. I went to the beauty shop and the grocery store or any other place on my agenda.

Even though Bob and the aide hit it off well together right from the start, he still wanted to keep a constant check on me. The beauty shop was my first stop, and I always called him on the car phone when I left there.

Then it wasn't long before he was calling me. He called me when I was at the local JCPenney store, at the grocery store, and at the gas station—mostly for reassurance. When I answered the phone, he would often ask me, "Where are you?"

"In the garage," I once replied, having just driven the car into the garage after my trip to the grocery store.

As Bob's condition worsened, I kept his sister in Kentucky informed of how he was doing. He and Barbie had been quite close while growing up. Bill, her husband, had been the educational director at a church in Lexington for almost as long as Bob and I had been married. In his tenure on the church staff, Bill had performed many funerals. He gave me a printed brochure called an Order of the Service. I could use Bob's picture on the cover and provide a lasting memorial.

When I shared my intention of giving the family eulogy myself, Barbie suggested that it might be easier for me if Bill did it. I liked that idea, and Bill agreed to it. I gave him a copy of what I had written, to use it as a guide. It was one more way God took care of my needs.

God also made spiritual provisions for me. He promises us in His Word that when we call to Him, He will answer (Jeremiah 33:3)—rather like a spiritual 911—and each day in one way or another the Lord came to my rescue. Sometimes it was a message in my daily devotional. Other times it was a song or a sermon on the Christian radio station. Often it was a card that came in the mail. Each day, every day, I felt the Lord's love and the assurance of His presence.

Standing on the promises that cannot fail,
When the howling storms of doubt and fear assail,
By the living Word of God I shall prevail,
Standing on the promises of God.[1]

Through that hymn God reminded me I could trust Him and stand on His promises.

As Bob's condition grew more critical and fatigue battered my body, a little plaque in our bedroom became my encourager. The letters burned into the wood said, "Keep me going, Lord."

Steve had sent the plaque to us several years before as a birthday present. I had seen the plaque hundreds of times, but during those difficult days it had a new meaning for me. Yes, God would keep me going—no matter what. For the first time, I *really* saw it.

God's help was there when I needed it. This is the way it was with

[1] Words and music by R. Kelso Carter, 1886.

all my "special messages." Seeing them at some other time, they would probably have had no significance, but when I needed help, they were very meaningful.

Writing down the ways God rescued me helped. A friend from church gave me a little oval-shaped box covered with golden ribbon and beige lace. She called it a "blessing box." Attached to it was this note:

> *When you're high atop the mountain*
> *And the world seems bright and clear,*
> *Why not write the Lord a thank-you note*
> *And place the pages here.*
> *And when the trials of life begin—*
> *Although you didn't ask it,*
> *Why not reach inside and count again*
> *The blessings in this basket (box).*

Writing down my blessings was a tangible reminder that when *I* draw near to God, *He* draws near to me (James 4:8).

God's phone line never gives a busy signal.

Chapter 12

Revive and Refurbish

[Jesus said], "Come ye yourselves apart into
a desert place, and rest a while."
Mark 6:31

Toward the end of July, Bob's memory became short and fragmented.
He could not remember what pills he had taken and if they had any
effect.

One day while talking to Steve on the phone, I shared this frustration with him. He suggested keeping a progress chart. I took his
advice and started keeping a record of how many pills Bob took each
day and how well they worked.

It worked fine for a few days, but then Bob couldn't understand it,
for it didn't lessen his agitation.

After a particularly frustrating morning, I shared my concern with
Nurse Gail that afternoon. As I talked with her on the patio, I
described the pressure of being asked the same thing over and over.

"You need to get away more often than Thursday mornings when
you run your errands," she said. "You're not superwoman or
supernurse. You need some time away by yourself. I'll see if the aide
can come more often."

When Gail put her arm around my shoulders, I could no longer keep back the tears I had been fighting. Her compassion broke through my defenses.

"This frustration is common with caregivers," Gail continued. "It's perfectly normal. It doesn't mean you don't love your husband, or you're not doing a good job. You just need some time for R and R. But rather than "rest and relaxation," we call it "revive and refurbish.""

Her understanding made me feel better. As I walked to the door with her, she told me volunteers were available to stay with Bob for several hours. They were usually older ladies. They had no special training but were available to sit with patients.

When I went back to Bob, he noticed my eyes were a little red and asked me about it. I explained to him that I had talked to Nurse Gail about my need to have a little time to myself. He didn't make any comment, but I sensed he was hurt that I wanted to be away from him.

That evening when Bonnie called, I told her about my afternoon conversations. "Don't feel guilty about it," she told me. "Everyone needs rest. You know, even Jesus took time to rest."

I had to smile at her reminder of a divine need.

She invited me to go to lunch with her the following Friday. "I have the day free, and Tom can stay with Bob," she said. "They'll have a good time talking about their old navy days." Since both Bob and Tom had been sailors in World War II, they always enjoyed swapping stories.

Rather reluctantly I agreed, trying not to feel guilty. When I put down the phone, I felt as if my spirit had been brushed with fresh air. Just having the prospect of a couple of hours' release made me feel so much better.

When I told Bob about the tentative plans, he said, "I know you need to get away."

We didn't talk anymore about it, but the next morning I realized he had been brooding about it all night. As soon as we finished breakfast, he said, "There's something I want you to do."

"What is it? I'll do anything I can."

"I want you to put me in a nursing home."

"Why?" I gasped. I wasn't prepared for anything like that, and I collapsed in a cloud of tears. "I don't want to put you in a nursing home. I love you. I want you right here beside me."

"Taking care of me is too much for you," he said, his voice tinged with courage.

In an effort to control my tears, I looked over to the dresser. There was a framed picture of a solitary red rose blooming through a crack in solid cement. Underneath was the caption: "Though I walk in the midst of trouble, thou wilt revive me" (Psalm 138:7).

The words and the picture spoke about God's promise of revival. The rose had persevered against overpowering odds—and had won the battle. At Bob's request, I had had the picture framed. He looked at it often, using it as a source of strength and a reminder of God's love and provision.

Now looking at the picture through my tears, I realized in a new and real way that God was right there with me in "the midst of my trouble," and He would "revive me."

"I want you to put me in a nursing home," Bob repeated. I knew he didn't mean it. I also realized he didn't understand my feelings of fatigue or my need for just a temporary relief—not a permanent release.

I called his attention to the picture as I took hold of his hand. "Just as God took care of the rose," I said, "He's going to take care of us. We're in this fight together. And we're going to stay together."

He squeezed my hand. He never again mentioned a nursing home.

The following Friday, Bonnie and I went to lunch. I enjoyed our conversation and the zucchini parmigiana that I ordered, but more than anything, I appreciated the freedom from my tether. The casual, noisy restaurant refreshed my frazzled spirit. On the advice of Nurse Gail, I left the car phone at home. I didn't realize till then how stressful it was to be constantly on the alert for a call.

After lunch I was anxious to go back home and be reassured that Bob was all right, but the time away was like a refreshing swim in a cool pond on a hot day.

This was just one more way in which God supplied my need.

An hour apart may be the best way to be together.

Chapter 13

Forty-Two Years and Holding

In every thing give thanks.
1 THESSALONIANS 5:18

Our forty-second wedding anniversary was the second of August. As that date drew near, I found myself both looking forward to and dreading it at the same time. What could I do to make that day special for the one I had lived with and loved for more than four decades?

When Bonnie called one night near the end of July, she said, "I know next week is your anniversary. And since you can't go out to dinner, Tom and I will bring dinner to you."

As we continued talking, she outlined a plan. They would not stay to eat with us. Anniversary dinners should be eaten alone, she explained, but they would supply the food.

After we finished talking, I told Bob about the arrangement. "Isn't that great?" I said. "We can have a special anniversary dinner together after all." I tried to sound happy and excited, hoping he would be pleased.

Bob turned his head away from me. Tears moistened his eyes. *"I can't do anything for you this year,"* he faltered.

In forty-two years, he had never once forgotten our anniversary.

Always he had taken me to dinner at a special restaurant and had a card and a small gift for me. I knew it hurt him deeply that this year he could do nothing.

As I took his hand, I cried too. "Honey, we're together," I said. "That's all that matters."

Our three grandchildren sent us a variety of pictures they had colored and papers they had decorated with stickers. They used a roll of paper to create their most important greetings. With Magic Markers two-year-old Kit decorated her section with long squiggly lines. Four-year-old Gwen did a watercolor painting of a blue flower with a red center, plus a few multicolored balls and a drawing of a bird or fish (I wasn't sure which).

Zachary pasted full-size sheets of pink and green construction paper on his part of the roll. In the precise printing of an eight-year-old on ruler-straight lines, he wrote the following message:

> Dear Mimi and Gampi—
>
> Congratulations! We hope you have a great day together on your anniversary. We wish we were there to help you celebrate. You are both a great example of Christian love to us. You are in our prayers. May God bless you on this special day.
>
> All our love,
> Zak, Gwen, and Kit.

I posted all the artwork on the wall.

Steve and Laura, as well as Gary and Dana, sent us cards that we stood up on the dresser beside Bob's bed. They also called us on the phone with anniversary greetings.

At noon Tom and Bonnie arrived with dinner: turkey breast with dressing, mixed vegetables, fruit salad, and pineapple upside-down cake. Pink-and-blue cloth place mats and special anniversary napkins added a festive touch. They even brought a centerpiece of fresh flowers and candles. We had all the trimmings of a special celebration— never mind that the candles couldn't be lit because of Bob's oxygen.

Tom and Bonnie also supplied us with cards for each other—one for each of us to give to the other. I knew they had chosen the cards carefully. The verses were lighthearted with a touch of humor but serious in their message of love.

I put Bob's dinner on his over-the-bed stand, and I sat on the opposite twin bed with a TV tray for my table. As we enjoyed our dinner, I tried to make light conversation and talk about the night of our wedding forty-two years before.

We had been married in Coral Gables, Florida, two days after I graduated from the University of Miami. We had chosen that date so my parents from Massachusetts could be there for both occasions.

"Remember how the police stopped us after our wedding reception when we were trying to get away?" I asked. "There were about a dozen cars following us with their horns honking."

"I remember," Bob said. "That cop sure was nice. When we told him the situation, he made everyone stay back until we drove out of sight."

I could still sense the apprehension remembering when Bob got out of the car to talk to the policeman. "I had visions of spending our first night in jail," I said, laughing. We laughed about it now, but it wasn't funny then.

Then there was the incident that took place when we were checking into the motel. While I waited in the car, Bob went inside to sign the registry. When he pulled out his wallet to pay for the room, a pocketful of rice fell onto the floor. The motel clerk smiled knowingly.

When we finished our anniversary dinner, I produced our wedding album and my bride's book. Together we reviewed pictures of the rainy night we were married. I had dressed in a room at the back of the church, then walked outside to the sanctuary. One of the pictures in the album showed Bob's best man and an usher holding a raincoat over my head as I lifted up my skirts to scurry up the stairs.

The day of our wedding there had been no breeze, and the air was like a sauna bath. This was before air-conditioning, and the church was stifling. As I walked down the aisle on my dad's arm, I was afraid Bob was going to faint before I got to the altar. He looked pale and was reeling a little. In the years that followed, he often used this as his excuse to kid me that he didn't know what he was doing that night.

Even though we both knew this would be our last anniversary together, the pain was kept at a minimum. By remembering the joy we had shared in the past, we were able to hurdle the pain of the present. It is the present in which God's grace is sufficient. As the poem says, His name is "I AM," not "I WAS" or "I WILL BE."

At the end of the day, I was tired—and thankful. Bob's mind had been comparatively clear, and medication had kept his pain quite well in check. As we focused on our shared love, our day of togetherness had been one of shared joy instead of the emotional hurt I had feared.

Sometimes blessings bloom in unexpected places.

Chapter 14

God's Perfect Timetable

It is appointed unto men once to die.
HEBREWS 9:27

Each day Bob's pain became worse. It was especially bad in the mornings. A few days after our anniversary, his pain was so bad he could hardly catch his breath. Even with pain pills, coping was becoming more difficult.

"Why won't God let me die?" he cried one morning as I prepared his breakfast.

"That's up to God," I told him, almost in a whisper. "We just have to trust Him."

"I've prayed for trust," he said. "Why can't I trust Him more?"

As I searched for words to help him, I remembered the Bible story of Peter walking on water. I asked Bob if he remembered it, and he said he did.

"As long as Peter kept his eyes on Jesus, he could stay on top of the water," I said. "When he looked at the waves, he went under. That's what we're doing. We're looking at the waves. We've got to keep our eyes on Jesus."

"I can't even pray anymore," Bob said.

"That's when the Holy Spirit prays for us," I answered. I said that as much for my own benefit as for his. Sometimes I, too, found praying difficult when I was tired and frustrated. Then I would realize I was watching the waves instead of keeping my eyes on Jesus.

Death was constantly on Bob's mind. *What will it be like to die?* he wondered. *Will I be in great pain? Will I suffocate? Will I die in my sleep?*

When he told me about his concern, I recalled a song I had heard at church. "Do you remember the song that says how wonderful it would be to go to sleep and wake up on the other side?" I asked.

> *Just think of stepping on shore and finding it heaven!*
> *Of touching a hand and finding it God's!*
> *Of breathing new air and finding it celestial!*
> *Of waking up in glory and finding it home!*[1]

Bob didn't reply then, but a few days later he said, "I'm ready to go. I've made my peace with God." Then he added, "Heaven must be a beautiful place."

That night he dreamed he couldn't get his breath, and he thought he was dying. When he related this to me the next morning, he told me he had said to himself, "This is it." Then he sensed the Lord's presence, and the message came to him clearly: "It will be when *I* am ready."

When Pastor Davies visited that afternoon, Bob told him about the dream. "Were you relieved or disappointed that you didn't die?" Pastor asked.

Bob considered the question; then he smiled and said, "A little of both."

As August wore on, Bob's breathing became more labored. Sometimes he didn't seem to be breathing at all for a couple of minutes. Then he would take several gasping breaths, and once again he would be breathing normally.

[1] Don Wyrtzen, *Finally Home*. Used by permission.

He was sleeping much more, but when he was awake, he was more agitated. He often told me he felt "fidgety." He would say he felt as if he was going to "jump out of his skin," and he would ask me for his "fidget pill." This was a tranquilizer that quieted his nerves and often made him sleep. Sleep became an avenue of escape.

As his confusion increased, he often insisted on getting out of bed, even though he was so weak he could hardly stand. He would throw his feet through the side rails and try to push himself under the rails to the floor. Then he would unbutton his shirt and attempt to take off his clothes.

Steve checked on his condition almost every day from California, and Gary called as often. Gary's job as a pilot required him to fly all over the country, so he called from some faraway places. Barbie, Bob's sister, also called frequently.

On Sunday, August 21, I awakened to find that Bob had soiled his bed and was so tangled in the covers I couldn't free him from his self-imposed prison. I called Tom and Bonnie, and in a few minutes they came to help me. Together we bathed him and made him as comfortable as possible. Tom shaved him. He and Bonnie stayed with me until Bob dozed off. They came back again after church that evening to help me get him settled for the night.

After I went to bed, I was awake till one in the morning trying to decide whom I might call for live-in help. Barbie had offered to come and stay with me, but she had recently had hip-replacement surgery. Laura had offered to come from California, but what would she do with the children? Having three children in the house would be no help. My process of elimination narrowed to Gary.

The next morning Bob woke me at five-thirty trying to crawl through the side rails. When I blocked his exit through the rails, he started pushing himself down the mattress toward the foot of the bed, mumbling incoherently. Not wanting to waken Tom and Bonnie at that hour, I tried to restrain him by myself, but not very successfully.

By six-thirty, he had successfully scooted down until his legs were over the end of the bed. Frantically I called Tom and Bonnie on the bedside phone. They came immediately—but to me it seemed like hours before they arrived.

Tom pulled Bob back onto the bed; then once again he and Bonnie helped me bathe him and change his linens. They stayed with me another hour till Bob was asleep, but I emphatically realized I needed more help than they could give me.

At seven-thirty, I phoned Gary to ask if he could take "family leave" and to come help me. He wasn't home when I called, but I left my frantic plea on his answering machine.

At noon Gary called from Washington, D.C. He was on a flight for the company. When I reiterated my need for help, he told me he would clear it with his boss and come home the following day.

When Nurse Gail came in the afternoon, I told her about my early morning problems.

"I think it's time you should have Thorazine suppositories to keep him calm," she said.

She phoned Bob's oncologist for the order, then called the pharmacy. After she left, my neighbor stayed with Bob a few minutes while I went to get the medication.

The Thorazine did help, and that night Bob slept a little better. The next morning Tom and Bonnie came again to help me give him his bath and shave him.

Bob slept most of the day. The only nourishment I could get him to take was a little juice and water. When Gary came that afternoon, I was never more glad to see anyone in all my life. I was so thankful that he had a job that allowed this time off and that he was willing to come.

During the night, Bob awakened me at one-thirty with difficulty breathing. His chest labored to take each breath. He gasped for air. I gave him Thorazine, but it didn't give him much relief. Then I remembered the morphine his oncologist had prescribed for breathing problems a few weeks earlier. It was a tiny white pill I could slip under his tongue. I was desperate to give him relief.

As I watched him struggle for air, I relinquished him to God. In my anguish, I cried, "Please, please take him home."

About three in the morning, Bob's breathing eased somewhat and he lapsed into a semi-coma. I fell exhausted into bed.

The next morning Tom and Bonnie arrived to help me; Gary remained in the basement where he had slept on the sofa bed. When he came upstairs, he handed me a letter he had started for his dad the night before and had finished that morning. As he handed it to me, he said, "Will you read it to Dad for me?"

"Why don't you read it yourself?" I asked.

"I want you to read it to him."

When I looked into Gary's eyes, I realized the emotional battle that confronted him. Handling emotions had always been difficult for him. I agreed to read the letter.

I pulled a chair up next to Bob's bed to be as near to him as possible, and holding his hand, I read the letter to him. I doubted he could hear me, but since hearing is our most acute sense, I hoped that he could.

Dear Dad:

In a couple of days it will be your birthday again. I wish so much that your sixty-eighth birthday could be a special day for you. I'm glad I'll be able to share it with you.

I know I have the reputation of being able to come up with unique gifts for special occasions, but for the first time in my life, I am really stumped as to what to give you—so I have decided to write a letter and share a part of myself with you. Dad, I know you'll never read this letter, and how I wish you could have one lucid moment where you could understand the things I'm trying to say. It's obvious I waited too long to do this, but hopefully you'll understand.

Dad, this is probably one of the most difficult things I've ever done. There is so much I want to say—and there is so much more that is felt but words cannot express—that I really don't know where to begin. First of all, I just want to say thanks for being my dad. Being a father involves a lot of things. It involves self-sacrifice, love, money, discipline, dedication, and involvement—to name just a few.

Growing up, it was virtually impossible to see the wisdom or motivation behind some of your decisions and actions. Yes, sometimes the discipline was too tough, or there were poor decisions that were made, but I thank God that you accepted the challenge of raising kids, stuck to your convictions, and made the difficult choices.

I'm thankful too that you didn't always let me have my way, and when appropriate, you let me fail sometimes. After every failure you were there to pick me up and encourage me to try again. Those are the things that growing up I had no understanding of or appreciation for.

I'd also like to apologize for every foolish argument, every immature action, and every time I disappointed you. I'm sure those moments caused you a lot of heartache and pain. If I could, I'd like to turn back the hands of time and change all that.

I'd also like to thank you for my Christian upbringing. I didn't always enjoy it; in fact, at times it was pretty embarrassing being the only kid on the block who went to church as much as I did. Once again, looking back I can see the positive impact it had on my life. I've walked away many times, but because of all your prayers and my upbringing, I've always come back. For that I can only say thank you.

You see, Dad, you'll never read this letter because tonight you slipped into a coma as a result of the bone cancer you've battled for the last twelve years. You fought the disease courageously; however, in time the end result was inevitable. Although I'm sure you had your moments of self-pity, not once did I hear you complain or ask, "Why me?" You just accepted it and kept going the best you could.

Death is a journey we all must make at one time or another. There is no convenient time to die! I'm just thankful for the gift of salvation and the promise of eternal life. I just want you to know that if it was within my power, I'd do anything I could to take this disease from you. I guess that is a selfish response on my part because I don't want to lose you. Not only are you my father, but over the years you've become my best friend. You've been a source of encouragement and understanding and unconditional love. How I wish that over the years I would have taken more time out of my schedule to spend more time with you—time to talk, to share, and to seek your guidance and advice.

Dad, I want you so much to be a part of future events in my life, but I know that will never happen. Even though the separation is temporary, I will miss you deeply. It's difficult to lose someone whom you love so much. Dad, I hope that you were as proud to have me as your son as I was to say that you were my father. Sometimes raising kids can be disappointing and include a lot of heartache. However, I hope to be as good an example of what a father and a husband means to my kids as you were to me!

However, on your birthday, I do have a request to make of you: When we are reunited in heaven, the first thing we'll do is play catch like we did so many times in the backyard.

Dad, I love you and will miss you dearly.

Happy Birthday.

Your son, Gary.

When I finished reading the letter, I felt as if my heart would break. I went out to the patio where Bonnie was waiting. She enveloped me in her arms and just held me while I cried.

How I wished Gary could have written that letter a month

before—or even a week before. Reading that letter would have meant so much to Bob. He always wanted to be the father he felt God would have him to be, but so often he felt he had failed. Maybe he did understand now. I prayed that he did.

When Pastor Davies visited after lunch, he said to Bob, "You have now run the twenty-sixth mile." And once again, I hoped Bob understood the message.

Dana came later that afternoon. She had come, as planned, to be with us for Bob's birthday the following day. Barbie and Bill also were coming the next day. In the evening I called to tell them of Bob's condition, and they said they would be with us as soon as possible.

The next morning, Bob's sixty-eighth birthday, Barbie and Bill arrived. They had been driving since 4 A.M.

Soon after they came, Bob was a little more alert than he had been. After the exchange of greetings with Bill and Barbie, Gary said, "It may seem a little strange, but let's sing 'Happy Birthday' to Dad."

We all stood around Bob's bed and sang "Happy Birthday." Then we showed him the birthday cards that had come and the gifts we had bought for him. He gave no conscious recognition of anything—but perhaps he knew.

At noontime we were eating an impromptu lunch of sandwiches and potato chips when we heard Bob moan. We exchanged questioning glances, and I rushed into the bedroom. As soon as I saw Bob, I realized his breathing was much more labored. Barbie followed me to his bedside and stood quietly beside him a few moments. When Gary came into the room, she left to help Dana clear away the lunch dishes.

Gary stood on one side of the bed, and I stood on the other. We each held one of Bob's hands. I glanced at the clock. It was 1:20. As we watched, Bob's breaths came less and less frequent. "I don't think it will be much longer," I whispered.

Each moment seemed like an eternity as we waited for the next breath. At 1:30 he gasped—and breathed no more.

He had gone home to be with his Lord for a much better birthday celebration. It was God's perfect timing. It was *His* appointment.

God counts time on His own calendar.

Chapter 15

The World Beyond

*I will strengthen thee; yea, I will help thee; yea, I will uphold
thee with the right hand of my righteousness.*

ISAIAH 41:10

The Bible assures us that being "absent from the body" is to be "present with the Lord" (2 Corinthians 5:8). With Bob's last breath, I knew without a doubt that he was with the Lord. The battle for him was over—the race had been won. Heaven must be a *wonderful* place.

But for me the battle was just beginning. Gary and I held Bob's hands a few seconds after he stopped breathing. We exchanged knowing glances and then tearfully embraced each other. Gary's strong arms around my shoulders gave me encouragement, but still the realization of being alone swept over me.

We went to the dining room. Barbie and Dana were still clearing the table from lunch. "He's gone," I said simply.

Barbie looked shocked. "I didn't think he would go that fast." Hurriedly she went into the bedroom.

I leaned back against the end of the dining-room table. In that instant, as time seemed to stop for me, it was almost like being suspended in space. Familiar things no longer seemed real.

"I suppose we have to make a few phone calls," I said.

Gary volunteered. As Nurse Gail had instructed me, he called her first. Then he called Pastor Davies at the church. Our next call was to Steve and Laura in California. They weren't at home, but Gary left a message on their answering machine. He called Tom and Bonnie, who offered to pick up anything that needed to go to the funeral home.

"Anyone else?" Gary asked.

"Please call Liz." She had been my friend for over thirty years. When Gary told her that Bob had died, she volunteered to call several of our other friends. She even called friends who had moved out of town.

Fifteen or twenty minutes later, Nurse Gail came. After she checked Bob to be certain death had indeed occurred, she phoned the oncologist. Because he knew so well the prognosis of Bob's illness and trusted the efficiency of hospice, he was willing to give the pronouncement of death over the phone. The official time that would appear on the death certificate was 2:05 P.M.

Pastor Davies arrived a few minutes later. The hospice program suggested that I not be in the house when Bob's body was taken to the funeral home. Bill helped Pastor Davies set up chairs on the lawn, facing away from the house. Gary and Barbie joined us, and we discussed the particulars of the funeral and other pertinent details with Pastor. The memorial service was set for Sunday with visitation hours the day before.

The obituary notice was already written, except for the dates of death and the services. We were able to quickly fill in the blanks. It would appear in the next day's newspaper. Tom and Bonnie took it to the funeral home for me, along with Bob's clothes and the collage I had prepared. Having all those details taken care of made everything so much easier.

There were other relatives to notify—aunts, cousins, nieces, and nephews—and within just a few hours, friends started to call to offer their condolences.

The next day was a blur of phone calls. Though they were appreciated, by afternoon they made me feel as if I was on a treadmill going nowhere. They were taking up all my time, and the house would be filled with guests arriving later that night.

Dana was an absolute lifesaver. She and Barbie took over the kitchen. As food from church friends and others started arriving, Dana took charge of everything. She didn't ask me what to do with anything—she just did it.

Gary helped her bring card tables down from the attic and set up a buffet on the patio. Later they went to the store to buy paper tablecloths and napkins. They called from the mall and asked me what Bob's favorite color had been.

"It was blue. Why do you want to know?"

"It's a surprise," Dana said.

When they returned home, they told me the light blue tablecloths and napkins were a tribute to Bob. Since he had been in the navy, they had also bought tiny clipper ships to decorate the tables.

Everything was ready and organized when Steve and Laura and the children arrived from California later that afternoon. That evening other relatives came from Kentucky, Georgia, and North Carolina. Laura's sister from West Virginia came to take care of the children. They stayed at a nearby hotel, but they ate with us.

Saturday morning Pastor Davies went with us to the funeral home for a private good-bye. As we approached the open casket, my throat felt tight and my mouth was dry. Although others were with me, it was as if I was in the room alone.

Bob's face bore a peaceful expression. His wedding ring that was still on his finger comforted me. Love enveloped me and thwarted my tears. Pastor Davies said a few words—I don't remember what they were—and he prayed with us.

I knew that soon after we left, the casket would be closed and sealed. This was my request so people would remember Bob as he was in life, not in death. Leaving the room seemed to shut that door with a harsh finality. I knew I would never see him again until we were together in heaven.

Visitation hours were later that afternoon. I had rather dreaded that time of meeting people, but God helped me through it with a strength that wasn't my own. Dana, Barbie, and Bill greeted people at the door, and Steve and Gary stood beside me as a long line of people filed by. Liz had thoughtfully supplied cold drinks, which was most helpful when my throat became dry from talking.

Although we had requested a memorial be made to our church in lieu of flowers, there were still several floral arrangements and plants. Steve and Laura supplied a large spray of white baby's breath and three red roses for the top of the closed casket, each rose representing one of their children. Gary and Dana provided pink and blue flowers to decorate the picture collage. On an easel next to the casket, I had a cross made of red roses and carnations with a ribbon reading "Loving Family." A separate little table held the framed poem that Jeff had given Bob. A solitary red rose rested beside it.

The following afternoon we had the memorial service in the church sanctuary. Instead of having the casket present, a large framed picture of Bob graced the front of the church. I intended the service to be a celebration of life—not a commemoration of death.

The printed order of service also had Bob's picture on the cover. His favorite poem, "Footprints," was inside, and on the back cover were the words to the song entitled "Victory in Jesus." Bob had especially liked this song, and several times he had requested that it be sung at his funeral. As a tribute to him, I was hoping the printed words would speak to anyone present who was not a believer.

For the prelude, a friend from our Sunday school class played a medley of Bob's favorite hymns on the piano. Bill delivered the family eulogy, quoting verbatim what I had so hurriedly typed into the computer the day after my sojourn to the cemetery.

Midway through the service, Dana sang "Amazing Grace." Then Pastor Davies delivered the memorial message. He spoke of the legacy of faith Bob had given to his sons. He told about the day Bob had said, "Pray I will be faithful to the end, and that I will be an example to others."

"The Lord answered both those requests," Pastor said. Then he told about the night Bob had cried out to the Lord, "God, why haven't you taken me home yet?" And what Bob said the next morning: "He's going to do it in *His* time."

Pastor referred to the little book Gary had given to his dad for Father's Day. He said Bob had proudly showed it to him one day when he was visiting. He quoted from it: "Dads are most ordinary men turned by love into adventurers, storytellers, and singers of songs. There is really a touch of magic in a dad. Dads can do anything."[1]

"Bob was fifteen years old when he made his commitment to the Lord," Pastor continued, "a good boy who realized he needed to be forgiven of his sins and invite the Lord Jesus Christ into his heart. That changed Bob's life—and that's what allows him now to enter into another part of God's creation, where he will live forever."

Pastor closed the service by sharing from letters Gary and Steve had written to their dad. He read first from the one Gary wrote for Bob's birthday in which he requested they would play catch in heaven like they had done so many times in the backyard.

Steve's letter was one he had written soon after his Easter visit but had never sent. As Pastor read from it, I wished that Steve had sent it. "To the very core of my soul," Pastor read, "to the very center of who I am, I believe we will be together again. There won't be any lawns to mow, and we'll just sit and talk. My love for you will last for eternity."

The service concluded with everyone standing to sing together "Victory in Jesus." Jesus was the one who gave Bob the victory.

The next morning our immediate family went to the grave site to say our last good-bye. We filed into the two rows of straight-back chairs by the grave. Several flower arrangements flanked the casket, and the spray of baby's breath and three roses rested on top.

[1]Pam Brown, *To a Very Special Dad* (Mt. Kisco, N.Y.: Exley Giftbooks, 1993).

The August sunshine touched us with a warm embrace. Pastor Davies read from the Bible and referred to the Scripture that had been God's message to me the morning Bob requested going to a nursing home: "Though I walk in the midst of trouble, thou wilt revive me" (Psalm 138:7).

Those same words were the featured verse in my daily devotional guide on the day Bob died. Again, it was God's message to me at a time when I most needed it.

The next morning Steve had to return to California to his job, and Dana went back to Columbus. Other relatives had left after the graveside service. Gary stayed with me a few more days, and Laura and the children stayed ten days to help me bridge the gap to a life alone.

I was so thankful for the strength, the stamina, and the peace of mind that God infused into me. We do, indeed, have a wonderful Lord who upholds us with the right hand of His righteousness—He never fails us.

Light shines brightest in dense darkness.

Chapter 16

Solo Venture

***[Jesus said], "Surely I am with you always,
to the very end of the age."***

MATTHEW 28:20, NIV

Realizing my time with Laura and the children was short, and faced
with the possibility of not seeing them again for several months, I
gave them my total attention. We spent a day shopping, went search-
ing for antiques, and played with the kids one afternoon at a park
where there were swings and a sandbox. Laura tried to keep my mind
focused on family and fun, but the many details of Bob's death and of
life alone plagued me.

When Laura and the children left to go to the airport, an overpowering sense of loneliness engulfed me. As they drove out of sight, I
reluctantly went into the house—the empty house.

The reality of being a widow assaulted me. The rooms seemed large
and so very quiet. And they were going to be empty and quiet from
now on. My life was going to be very different from what it had been.
Would I be able to cope?

In the kitchen, a round magnet on the refrigerator door caught my attention. It pictured two deer splashing through a shallow country stream. Beside them in bold black letters was this message: "Lord, help me remember that nothing is going to happen today that You and I can't handle."

Thank-you notes had to be written, insurance companies notified, credit cards changed, the lawyer contacted. I didn't know where to begin.

Checking the mail that had accumulated in an empty drawer seemed like the best place to start. Sympathy cards tumbled over unopened bills and advertisements. After throwing out the ads and piling up the bills, opening the cards became my first objective.

Each card was a personal message from the friend who had sent it—and from the Lord. Many of the verses assured me of God's presence and guidance. Several people included a clipping of the obituary.

Using the notepaper the funeral home supplied, I sent notes of gratitude to everyone who had sent flowers, brought food to the house, or made contributions to the church in Bob's memory. Legal things needed attention. Our lawyer would settle the estate, and I would need to write a new will. Bank accounts had to be changed to my name. Bob's monthly social-security check needed to be sent to me.

Some days my head ached from the muddle. Keeping a to-do list and checking off the tasks as they were accomplished helped. Just as God gives us strength one day at a time, He likewise gives us ability to handle our problems one at a time.

Philippians 4:13 became very real to me: "I can do all things through Christ which strengtheneth me." Whenever I sat down at the writing desk, I reread the clipping from the church bulletin quoting from the song "Because He Lives":

> *Because He lives I can face tomorrow,*
> *Because He lives all fear is gone;*
> *Because I know He holds the future.*
> *And life is worth the living just because He lives.*

Returning as quickly as possible to my normal routine of life was a
great help. Numerous church activities, an early morning aerobics
class, time spent with friends—all were part of the healing. I joined
the Toastmasters, a group dedicated to learning public-speaking efficiency. I began to attend a Bible study, and each activity stretched my
horizons.

I chose to be busy and focus on the present instead of the past.
Staying home and feeling sorry for myself would have been easy but
would have accomplished nothing.

I decided to spend the first hour of my day with the Lord: reading
His Word and talking to Him in prayer. As the dark corners of my life
became illuminated with His presence, coping with the empty house
and the quiet rooms became easier.

I still had difficult moments. Often little things tripped me up.
Lemon meringue pie, Bob's favorite, evoked the memory of our
meals together. Coming across an empty box brought another memory.

One Easter Bob had given me an empty one-inch-square box
wrapped in blue paper and ribbon. Attached to it was the following
poem.

This is a very special gift
That you can never see.
The reason it's so special is
It comes to you from me.
Whenever you are lonely
Or even feeling blue,
You only have to hold this gift
And know I think of you.
You never can unwrap it—
Please leave the ribbon tied.
Just hold the box up to your heart
It's filled with love inside.

The most difficult hurdle came at church when the congregation stood to sing "Victory in Jesus." All the memories of the funeral flooded back to me. Tears burned in my eyes.

"Please God, don't let me cry." And I didn't. In little hurts, as well as the big ones, He was there to help me.

For my birthday in September, Gary invited me to spend a few days with him in Columbus. The prospect of driving there alone made me panic. It was only a two-hour drive on a well-marked four-lane highway, but Bob had always done the driving. Now *I* would have to read the map, watch the road signs, and make sure the car had enough gas.

Just before leaving, I paused to read the message on the refrigerator-door magnet: "Lord, help me remember that nothing is going to happen today that You and I can't handle." Driving to Columbus was the first of many accomplishments in which He would give His help.

Gary knew my birthday would be difficult, and he tried to fill the ensuing days with activity. Dana wanted to do her part, too. On the night of my actual birthday, she invited us to a candlelight dinner at her condo. Her mother came, too, and with all of us together, there was little time to think about the one I sorely missed.

Back home, as free time became available, I found joy in reaching out to other people: a meal cooked for a sick friend, a visit to an elderly shut-in from our church. There is never a lack of ways to help someone.

Holidays are particularly difficult to face alone. Somehow the house gets larger, more empty and more quiet then. I was thankful Steve and Laura invited me to spend two weeks around Thanksgiving with them in California, and Gary asked me to spend Christmas with him in Columbus.

That Christmas was very special for Gary and Dana, for it was then he officially asked her to marry him. Christmas morning Gary had her ring gift-wrapped under the tree. Dana carefully untied the bow and pulled apart the paper. Inside the package she found the beautiful ruby ring she and Gary had previously selected.

Gary knelt down in front of her, amidst the packages and wrappings, and asked her to marry him. I had the camera ready and snapped his picture.

"I will," Dana said. "I want to spend every moment of my life with you." Those were her exact words.

After returning home, I sent Dana a five-by-seven framed enlargement of Gary on his knees, with an attached note that read, "He can never say he didn't ask you."

Their wedding was set for the following April. At the rehearsal dinner, Dana presented gifts to her attendants, then read the note that Bob had written to her several months before: "To Dana—I do not know how long God has given me, but I can't consider any better choice for my son's life than you."

It seemed as if Bob had given his sanction to their union beforehand. I wished so much he could have been with us that evening, but I was thankful he had at least met Dana and had, in his own way, welcomed her to the family.

Steve and Laura came for the April wedding. Tom and Bonnie, Bill and Barbie were with us. It was a time of fellowship and joy.

When Gary and Dana had become engaged, he told me he had two requests regarding the wedding: he wanted to be married in his dad's blue serge suit, and he wanted Bob's picture beside him at the altar when he said his vows. Both requests were carried out. Bill, Bob's brother-in-law, performed the ceremony.

When the reception was almost over, Gary asked me to put some of the flowers from the wedding on Bob's grave. The next day when I returned home, I went directly to the cemetery.

A spring warmth blanketed the area, and the grass was beginning to turn green. A slight breeze moved the leaves of the white birch tree at the edge of the lawn beside the road. The world seemed fresh—and quiet—as I stood beside Bob's grave.

I felt as if a chapter of my life had been completed. Memories are a precious blessing—but life is for the living. And I could honor Bob's memory best by living life to its fullest.

A solitary journey is never lonely when traveled with the Lord.

Chapter 17

The Clipper's Healing Balm

Give, and it will be given to you. . . . For with the measure you use,
it will be measured to you.

LUKE 6:38, NIV

As the first anniversary of Bob's death drew near, tears were always
near the surface. Every time anyone reminded me of the difficult day
ahead, I cried.

Two weeks before that anniversary date, Tom and Bonnie said to
me, "We know August 25 is coming up. We'd like to take you out to a
late lunch, then go to a concert in the park."

I wasn't prepared for their offer. "Let me think about it," I said,
turning my head aside.

As the day drew nearer, the uncontrolled surge of tears was
repeated often. Both Steve and Gary called to tell me they would be
thinking of me and praying for me on that date. Friends at church told
me likewise. Pastor Davies and the church staff sent a card expressing
their concern for me.

I dreaded the day and wished that date could be erased from the calendar. On the morning of August 25, I prayed that God would help me

get through the day. This day was almost more difficult for me than the actual day Bob died.

I just wanted to be alone, not even talk to anyone. Twice when the phone rang I ignored it. My recorder told me it was Steve calling from California and Barbie phoning from Kentucky. I had already told Tom and Bonnie I would rather not go out to lunch or attend the concert. There was no way my mind could be tricked into not knowing what day it was.

As soon as the florist shop opened, I purchased a bouquet of flowers to put on Bob's grave. The red and white carnations reminded me of the flower spray near his casket with the "Loving Family" banner spread across it.

I drove to the cemetery in the bright August sunshine. I parked near a white birch tree that was near the grave.

Crabgrass hugged the perimeter of the grave, and weeds encroached upon the marker. The permanent metal vase implanted in front of the marker was totally obscured. I hadn't been back to the grave since early spring, and the effects of the lack of mainte-nance surprised me.

I returned home. After lunch I went back to the cemetery with clip-pers and garden gloves. I clipped away at the weeds by the marker. I began to feel my depression lifting. In a strange way it was almost like doing a service for Bob. Since he had died on his birthday, I felt this was my birthday gift to him.

The sky was blue. Trees offered their cooling breeze. A swish of a nearby sprinkler was the only sound that disturbed the solitude as I worked.

By the time I finished clipping, it was almost one-thirty—the exact time Bob had died a year earlier.

"Honey, I love you," I said, wishing he could hear me.

I gathered my gardening tools and went back to the car. As I drove away from the cemetery, I felt relieved of sorrow and able to face my world.

God had granted me peace and composure. He had assuaged my gloom and once again made me realize that happiness is found in service to others.

As we empty ourselves for others, God fills the vacuum with joy.

PART TWO

Caregiver Concerns

Chapter 18

Creating a Memory

As holidays and special events punctuate the calendar, make each one an occasion for a limited celebration. Do you have a special occasion you and your loved one who is terminally ill can share together? If you do, don't ignore or shy away from observing this special day. Enjoy it in a tender, creative way. Accept it as an opportunity to craft a precious memory that will always be cherished.

Special Occasions and Holidays

Family reunion: If the one you love is facing a terminal illness, you will find that time becomes precious as you realize it is fleeting. If your family is scattered, a family reunion would be a treasured event before your loved one becomes more ill. A family picture can become a priceless possession.

Small party: Perhaps you can plan a small party for your loved one; it doesn't have to be elaborate. If family isn't available, maybe you can invite a few friends for a simple luncheon. Even a quick visit of only a few minutes might make the day seem special. If possible, incorporate your loved one in plans for the day. Maybe he or she could peel some carrots for a relish tray, fold napkins, or help plan a menu.

Home entertainment: Perhaps you can make the day special by watching a rented movie together or viewing a home video that depicted that same holiday at an earlier time. Maybe your loved one would like to play a special board game such as checkers or would enjoy having you read aloud. Sections of the *Reader's Digest* such as "Life in These United States" or "Campus Comedy" are always fun to share. Be creative.

Birthday celebration: On your own or your loved one's birthday, you can remember the good times you have had together and express thanks for the years of life God has granted you. Perhaps your loved one could relate some little-known facts of his or her childhood; nostalgia can evoke happy memories.

If you aren't able to give your loved one a birthday cake because of diabetes or some other medical problem, perhaps you could simulate a cake made of sugar-free Jell-o. Or stick a candle in a dish of applesauce. It's the celebration that counts, not the ingredients that compose it.

Christmas observance: At Christmas you could share the joy of Jesus' birth and relive pleasant memories of other Yuletides.

A large decorated Christmas tree might seem prohibitive or objectionable, but you could give the bedroom a festive touch by having a small artificial tree on a bedside stand or dresser. You might want to add poinsettias, mistletoe, or other holiday decorations. If possible, encourage your loved one to help you make homemade decorations, such as a chain of interlocking red and green paper rings. Strings made of popcorn might be fun to make.

You might want to have your loved one help you wrap gifts. Even simple tasks like cutting ribbons or handing you pieces of tape will make him or her feel a part of the festivities.

Include children or grandchildren: If you have young children or grandchildren, try to make them part of your celebration. Not only will you be providing them with a happy memory, but you will be helping them bridge the gap between life and death.

faye landrum

Perhaps they could make a book for your loved one, expressing their love and telling how he or she has been special to them. This would make a cherished birthday or Christmas gift for your loved one, and the children or grandchildren will feel they have contributed to the joy of the occasion.

Memorabilia and Remembrances

Christian remembrances: If your loved one has been involved in ministry in any capacity, remind him or her of each endeavor and what was accomplished. Perhaps a plaque or some other tangible recognition could be displayed. To be remembered for service to our Savior is a legacy all Christians would like to leave.

Personal remembrances: We also would like to be remembered in a personal way by family and friends after we are gone. Perhaps your loved one could write a note to each member of the family. Or maybe he would rather use a tape recorder and say a few words or sing a song to each one.

A recording of a family holiday spent together, such as Christmas, can be a treasured memory.

Memorabilia remembrances: Is there jewelry, furniture, a stamp collection, or some other item that has special meaning to you or your loved one that you want to designate for a certain person?

If your loved one has a prized possession he or she wants someone special to receive, encourage him or her to give it early on. That way your loved one can experience the joy of sharing it with that person, and it would still be a legacy for years to come.

Bible legacy: A personal Bible can be an inherited treasure. Underlined passages and personal notes in the margins are like a road map of one's life.

Chapter 19

Causes of Stress

The grind of continual care with no relief in sight is often the worst phase of caregiving. Most of us are used to busy, full lives, and cabin fever can be maddening. After a while stress can show on the caregiver, and your feelings may whirl as mine did.

Guilt

As fatigue overtakes you, you may want to get away. You have no time to do anything *you* want to do; even phone calls are interrupted. You wish the agony were over, and then you realize the only way it will end will be with the death of your loved one. Shocked at your own feelings, you think, *How can I feel that way?*

Every caregiver has these thoughts. It's not a sign that you lack love or commitment; it's a sign that you're human, and self-indulgence is an ever-present sin we all must battle.

You may ask yourself, "Am I doing enough?" Then guilt rages within you because inside, you wish you were doing less.

You may hesitate to leave your loved one with someone else. Guilt dictates, "If something happens and I'm not there, it will be my fault."

Could you ever forgive yourself? And would others think less of you because you weren't there?

Guilt makes you wonder if people think you are as kind as you should be, attentive enough, or doing *all you can* to save the life of your loved one.

As you run up bills for treatments that aren't helping, you realize you are spending money you don't have. When you try to conserve, knowing you may need that money when you are left alone, guilt haunts you that you are being selfish.

Loneliness

Loneliness may stalk you. Everyone else appears to be *free*—but not you. You question where all your friends are (your "free" friends). How can you fill the long days when all you have to focus on are issues of illness: pain, nausea, and poor appetite? You are frustrated when your loved one won't eat, no matter how hard you try to fix favorite foods.

You question whom you can talk to who would be willing to come into your world, share your pain, love you anyway—and wouldn't feel you were a bother, or mind the sacrifice that a friendship with you would now entail.

Inadequacy

You possibly feel inadequate as you take over household chores that used to be done by your loved one. Men may find cooking a challenge they do not appreciate and ironing a task impossible to accomplish. Women may perceive the lawn mower as a menacing dragon in the shed and see gutters clogged with fall leaves as an insurmountable responsibility.

Fear

Fear may permeate your thoughts as you consider facing life alone. How will you manage without your best friend—your adviser (if finances are a mystery or are overwhelming), and your counselor (if family problems exist)? Does this loss mean you will never again feel loving arms around you? You may panic as you face these prospects.

Resentment

Then there is resentment. "Why me, God?" you may ask. You may resent everyone who has a healthy mate. You may even have resentment toward your loved one for getting sick; although it may be buried and you know it is irrational, it is still there. Then you want to scream, "How can I think like that?!"

Chapter 20

How to Handle Stress

Emotional Release

Sometimes it helps to cry; don't be ashamed if you do. Tears seem to wash away frustration like a spring rain cleanses the atmosphere. They are nature's way of relieving tension.

Time Away

If your loved one is still mobile, many cities have day-care centers that cater to the elderly and sick. Having some time away from home can be enjoyable for your loved one and profitable for you.

Try to carve out some time each day that you can claim for yourself. Maybe it's doing a crossword puzzle or a jigsaw puzzle—something you can enjoy in just snatches of time. You need little pieces of freedom without the guilt this respite might produce. Sometimes it takes an objective outsider, like a hospice nurse, to help you reconcile with this and to support you. Burnout is terrible but unavoidable. If you are going to go the whole distance with your loved one at home, you have to be wise *before* it happens.

Needed Rest

Occasionally you may want to ask someone to stay overnight so you can have eight hours of uninterrupted sleep. As Shakespeare noted: "Sleep . . . knits up the ravell'd sleave of care." Health-care agencies have "sitters" available who do not give nursing care but are able to attend to the simple needs of patients.

If your family or friends want to give you a gift for a special occasion, you might want to suggest they give you a night's rest by paying for a sitter. If you have adult children, maybe they would offer overnight relief for you. Do you have a friend or relative who can give you assistance? Most Christians would rather give help than receive it, but don't be too proud to ask for and accept the support of others. Realize that God may be using people as part of His provision for your needs—your psychological and spiritual needs as well as your physical ones.

Communication

Most friends truly want to help, but sometimes they feel awkward because they don't know what to do. You get the familiar "call me if you need anything." Don't be afraid to assign these friends a chore or duty—they are usually pleased to be able to help you. Usually friends feel powerless, but they appreciate being able to help and realize they were able to make a difference.

Friendship

Talking to a friend helps relieve the tension of being a constant caregiver. Although you may hesitate to burden others with your problems, seek out a friend with whom you can share your concern. Even just a few minutes of phone contact is helpful, and the fringe benefit is a deepening relationship for both of you.

Personal Touch

Perhaps there is something your loved one can do for you personally, such as rubbing your back or massaging your shoulders to relieve tension. If there is some intimate touch like this that you may have shared in the past, its continuance will help you to relax and help your loved one feel that he or she is still needed at the present time.

Spiritual Help

The stress of caring for a terminally ill loved one will either draw you closer to God or push you away from Him. When we watch a beautiful sunset with vivid colors reflected in the placid waters of an ocean harbor, it is easy to sense the presence of God. It is not as easy when fierce tempest winds tear apart our dwelling and angry waves threaten to engulf the shoreline. But the same Lord is there in both situations.

As you consider the illness of your loved one and contemplate the possibility of his or her encroaching death, God may seem a long way off. Even if you are a Christian, you may feel you cannot reach Him. A daily devotional calendar, found in Christian bookstores, may help you. If it is set in a prominent place, such as the counter near the kitchen sink, it will be a frequent reminder to you of God's strength and provision.

If you are not a Christian, but you would like to meet Jesus Christ, turn to the Bible. The book of John is a good place to start. Read it a couple of times, and ask God to help you understand it—and He will.

Keep a journal: If the weight of your loved one's illness is pulling you down, I would encourage you to keep a journal. Jot down the positive things that happen to you each day, not just the negative. Maybe the beauty of a cardinal feasting at your bird feeder refreshes you, or specks of dust dancing in a sunbeam amuse you. Jotting down just a simple word or sentence—something that doesn't take a lot of time—will make you aware that good things do occur and will help you search for them each day.

Look for ways the Lord comforts you. Sometimes in the rush of agony we neglect to notice the little blessings God has for us. Keeping a short diary will help you to be alert to His love and reassurance. As you look back over your entries, you will be amazed at His answers for your fervent pleas.

Electronic resources: As I mentioned before, it helps if you can be tuned in to God's resources, such as a Christian radio program or TV show. If that isn't available, playing a CD of classical music might be soothing, and a TV program or video of light comedy might relieve tension.

Prayer solace: Don't discount the solace of prayer. Talk to the Lord. Complain to Him if you want to—He knows how you feel anyway. Even if you pray silently while you are doing other tasks, be assured that God hears you. Listen for His answers.

Sometimes God's answers come in practical ways, such as in gifts of baby monitors and car phones. Maybe He will unexpectedly send you a friend, or rescue you in some other way. His relief may not be *all* spiritual.

Biblical help and balm: If possible, find time each day when you can be alone with the Lord and read His Word. You may find the Psalms especially beneficial. Reading how David shared his problems with the Lord may help you do likewise. We struggle for answers and have to admit that sometimes there are none. We may even ask, *Does Jesus care?* The following thoughts and Scriptures are drawn from a sermon by Pastor Davies regarding the tragedies that touch our lives. I hope they will be helpful to you.

- Psalm 116:15: "Precious in the sight of the Lord is the death of his saints" (NIV).

  God has a different perspective than we do about death. To us death is negative, but not to God. To us it means separation, but to God it means that we are ushered into the joy of His presence if we are believers.

- Isaiah 43:1-2: "Fear not, for I have redeemed you; I have summoned you by name; you are mine. When you pass through the waters, I will be with you; and when you pass through the rivers, they will not sweep over you" (NIV).

The allusion here is to the children of Israel in the wilderness, but it is also an assurance to us of God's nearness and His desire to help. We may feel God is a million miles away, but He tells us He is with us.

- John 16:33: "I have told you . . . that in me you may have peace. In this world you will have trouble. But take heart! I have overcome the world" (NIV).

  Jesus warned us that trials and problems are to be expected as a part of life, but if we turn to Him, we will find the comfort and peace we are seeking. We need to look beyond the immediate.

- Revelation 7:17: "For the Lamb which is in the midst of the throne shall feed them, and shall lead them into living fountains of waters: and God shall wipe away all tears from their eyes."

  There is a day coming when all pain and suffering will end. Does that take away the pain now? The answer is No. But it helps to realize that Jesus does care.

Self-Esteem

Reservoir of strength: As you look back over the past few days, weeks, or months, have you found strength you didn't know you possessed or compassion you didn't know you were capable of feeling? In the Old Testament, God gave the Israelites food in the form of manna one day at a time. Likewise He gives us strength one day at a time.

Don't be concerned about what you may have to face tomorrow. When tomorrow becomes today, trust God that the strength you need will be there.

Check Accomplishments: Take pleasure in the accomplishment of simple tasks, such as helping your loved one be more comfortable. Aren't fresh sheets on the bed rewarding?

Perhaps that letter you wanted to write, you were finally able to get in the mail. Maybe you succeeded in finding time to write checks for the bills that needed to be paid. Take note of such finished chores that otherwise might be easily overlooked as accomplishments. Remember that what you are doing *is* important.

Set little goals for yourself each day, reasonable things you can achieve by the time you go to bed at night. Just as a flight of stairs is climbed one step at a time, so big goals are realized by finishing little tasks one at a time.

Chapter 21

Medical Concerns

Doctor Visits

Do not be afraid to take up your doctor's time. If you have just received a serious diagnosis, make a list of your questions and concerns and schedule another appointment as soon as possible. This will help to relieve your anxiety. Most people usually remember very little from that first appointment when they receive a troubling prognosis.

If the diagnosis is cancer: The American Cancer Society recommends that *every* cancer patient be seen by an oncologist, even if he or she doesn't plan to receive treatment. An oncologist is much more knowledgeable in the field than other physicians and can be your best ally. If treatments (chemotherapy or radiation) are ordered, *read* the material given to you. Ask a medical professional to describe in detail what your loved one will experience and what you should do if and when problems arise. Don't be afraid to ask for medications to control symptoms or to request information on alternative forms of treatment. It is wise to keep yourself well informed of all the treatments and remedies available.

Ask and write out questions: As your loved one's illness progresses, continue to ask your doctor open, to-the-point questions. Some doctors have a hard time relaying bad news unless you ask them directly. Your loved one needs to have a doctor who will answer inquiries and be honest with you. Writing out your questions before your appointments will be helpful. Give them to the nurse when you go into the office so the doctor can be prepared when he or she sees you.

RN help: Get acquainted with the RNs in your oncologist's office. They can be your friends. If you establish a good rapport with them, you can call them when problems arise, which is more satisfactory than talking to the receptionist. Often a nurse can answer many questions that come up without even consulting the doctor.

Take notes: Take notes on your doctor's instructions during your loved one's appointments. Most people remember about half of what they hear because of their stress. It is important to understand and follow your doctor's advice to the best of your ability.

Doctor relationship: If you think your doctor is not a good match for you, ask people (especially those with medical expertise) to recommend another physician who might better fit your situation or personality. Having a close relationship with your doctor and respecting his or her advice is important. This gives you a sense of security as you have confidence in the course of treatment.

List medications: Keep a list of all current medications, both ongoing and temporary. Clip the list to the medical card, or whatever your loved one uses when he or she sees the doctor, so the information will be handy. The office personnel will appreciate this consideration of the time this courtesy saves.

Hospice Care

If the condition of your loved one has progressed to where he or she is considered terminal, which is usually defined as a life expectancy of six months or less, it may be time to call hospice.

Purpose: The purpose of hospice care is to provide comfort and the best possible quality of life to patients whose condition no longer warrants the pursuit of a cure. This is called *palliative* care, deriving from Greek and Roman times when men wore a pallium, which was a cloak or large covering. The idea behind palliative treatment is that it covers the patient with comfort care but makes no attempt to restore health.

Hospice does not take the place of your doctor; all personnel follow the doctor's orders and directions.

History: Hospices originated in the Middle Ages when Christians provided way stations for travelers. Many times the people who came to them were very ill or dying. The modern hospice movement started with Cecily Saunders, a Christian physician in Britain. She was first a social worker, then a nurse, and finally, a doctor. Still living today, she has started palliative care units and hospices around the world.

Usually hospices are freestanding establishments separate from hospitals, while palliative-care units are designated sections within medical facilities. They work together quite well because some people need hospice care at home while others need twenty-four-hour nursing care in a medical facility for regulation of pain control or other problems.

Nurses: A hospice can provide compassionate nurses who are experienced in the terminal process. They can help minimize your loved one's symptoms, answer your questions, and provide the instructions you need for giving care.

Social workers: Social workers can help if any type of hired continuous care is needed in your home or if placement of your loved one in an outside care facility is necessary.

Other specialists: Dietitians, therapists, volunteers, and clergy can also provide support for your individual needs at home. Nursing aides can help with baths, linen changes, and respite (time that allows you to get out of the house). All team members are qualified to help with emotional support.

Several different organizations may provide hospice care.

Please reference Chapter 24, "Helpful Organizations," for further information.

Home Care

Caring for your loved one at home can be challenging. Here is some advice to make your job a little easier.

Poor appetite: If poor appetite is a problem, try giving a high-calorie, high-protein diet in six small meals a day instead of the usual three larger ones. Avoid foods that need a lot of chewing. Give your loved one the freedom of knowing that everything on the plate doesn't *have* to be eaten.

Allow your loved one to have the privilege of eating anything that sounds good. Maybe it's a chocolate lollipop or potato chips—it doesn't matter. Liquid food supplements may be given. Ask a dietitian at the hospital or one with the visiting nurse service for pamphlets on diet suggestions. Don't force your loved one to eat. If you do, he or she may become sick. Sometimes cooking odors will cause nausea or lack of appetite. If the same food is cooked elsewhere, however, and brought in, it may be more acceptable.

Dry mouth: Dry mouth can be aggravating, but don't use a commercial mouthwash. One-half cup of warm water mixed with a half teaspoon of baking soda gives much more relief. If the mouth becomes dark red or white patches appear inside the mouth, tell your doctor or nurse.

Nausea: If your loved one has nausea, your doctor can order medications that will help. An unwanted side effect of the medication, however, may be drowsiness.

Constipation: Constipation can be agonizing. Relief may be difficult, but there are drugs that can help. Anyone on pain pills needs to have a bowel movement at least every other day; don't let this go or you will regret it. The higher the dosage of pain pills, the more laxatives are needed.

Skin irritation: For skin redness, Bag Balm (obtainable at the drugstore) is helpful if no irritation of skin is noted. If sores are present or the skin is peeling, a professional evaluation and a treatment plan are needed.

Self-Esteem: Low self-esteem is a crippling malady, but a sense of accomplishment can be an effective antidote. If you can devise a simple task or service your loved one can accomplish, you might be able to alleviate encroaching depression.

Doing crafts can be as enjoyable for men as for women. I had an uncle who learned to knit when he became incapacitated, and I had a male friend who took pride in fashioning lamp shades from Styrofoam containers and colorful beads.

At gift-giving time, such as a birthday or Christmas, you might encourage your loved one to produce some family presents. Even learning to paint by numbers might be an option, and a handcrafted picture would be a prized possession for a son or daughter.

Is there some easily accomplished task or service your loved one can do for you? It might be something as unpretentious as helping to fold the laundry, rearranging the bookshelf, or dusting the piano keys—anything that can give the satisfaction of a job completed.

Medical Equipment

The following medical equipment is commonly supplied by hospice: a hospital bed (makes care easier, elevates the patient's head for shortness of breath, and provides rails for safety); a walker (steadies the patient and prevents falls); a bedside commode (provided when walking to the bathroom causes severe fatigue or shortness of breath); a wheelchair (given to avoid exhaustion, fatigue, and falls); a foam pad for chair or bed (helps prevent bedsores); oxygen (for shortness of breath). All equipment must have medical approval.

Bedroom arrangement: A bedroom and bathroom on the first floor is ideal for patient care, but your home may be different. If your bathroom is upstairs, you may want the hospital bed set up in a downstairs family room with a commode nearby. Maintaining an upstairs bedroom is often difficult, for your loved one then feels isolated when not a part of family activities such as meal preparation. As the illness progresses and demands on caregiving increase, running up and down the stairs could easily exhaust you.

If you sleep in a double bed, you may want to dismantle it and have a rollaway bed for you next to the hospital bed.

Other resources: If hospice care is not available or advisable, other resources may be implemented. Hospital-type equipment may be rented. Even a motorized stair lift, although very expensive, may be either rented or purchased if an upstairs bedroom is used and you want access to the first floor.

Pain Control

Today pain control is sophisticated, and there are many options. If increased pain for your loved one is a problem, don't hesitate to ask your physician for added relief.

Analyze the pain: Have your loved one rate his or her pain on a scale of 1 to 10 (10 being most severe). If above two, call your doctor for medication that will give relief.

Regarding addiction: Do not be concerned about drug addiction. According to Dr. Margaret Cottle, a hospice physician from Canada and a member of the Focus on the Family Physicians Resource Council, palliative-care patients rarely become addicted unless they had an addiction problem in the past. Pain is an antidote to addiction. If pain decreases, the pain medication can be decreased also.

Medication dosage: Patients should not fear starting on stronger medications if unrelieved pain indicates they need them. There is no need to feel that stronger medications have to be saved until later, because there is no top dosage to strong pain medications. Nearly all pain can be controlled.

Types of medication: Needles are rarely used now for giving drugs to relieve pain. Pain medication is, instead, absorbed through the skin using a narcotic patch. More frequently, oral medications are used. Some types are even dissolved under the tongue. If stomach problems exist, long-acting rectal medications may be given every twelve hours. If none of these options are feasible, a tiny needle under the skin may be left in place as long as a week, and medication can be administered intravenously through a little rubber stopper by a hospice-care nurse or family member.

Nursing Home Considerations

Every situation is different. If you need the help of a nursing home, don't feel guilty about it. Accept it as one of God's provisions.

Facility availability: Many things need to be considered when opting for long-term care. First of all, you need to know what facilities are available in or near your community. Ask the advice of your doctor and consult friends who have had experience with them.

Visit facilities: Visit several of the homes and talk with the staff and management. Is there a stale or unpleasant odor, or a heavily perfumed odor obviously designed to mask the smells? Are the rooms clean and the halls free of clutter? Are bathrooms and shower rooms outfitted with handrails? Are the doors wide enough to accommodate wheelchairs? Is a nurse call button within easy reach? Do drapes or screens afford privacy in rooms designed for more than one patient? Is there adequate space for clothes and personal belongings? Are the rooms airy and pleasant? Is there air conditioning?

Check on meals: Try to be present during a meal. Is the food hot and appetizing? Is there adequate staff to give assistance if needed? Does the facility employ a registered dietitian? Are special dietary considerations available? Are fresh fruits and vegetables served instead of canned goods?

Miscellaneous provisions: Is there a beauty salon or barber shop on the premises? Is physical, occupational, speech or respiratory therapy available if needed? Is there a weekly nondenominational worship service? Are such fringe benefits as arts and crafts or exercise classes provided for those who can use them?

Is there a social worker on staff to help with procuring such specialized needs as prostheses, walkers, and wheelchairs? What is the emotional climate of the facility? Do the patients seem contented?

Financial considerations: Finances need to be considered. Will you be able to afford the monthly payments? What about Medicare or Medicaid? You need to check out the rules because they are constantly changing.

Are there hidden costs, such as laundry service? Who pays for prescriptions and items such as diapers and nutritional supplements?

In summary, don't be afraid to ask questions.

Finances

Medicaid: Medicaid is a program of federal and state assistance for those needing medical care who have physical limitations (blind, disabled, or over 65) and are without certain resources or available income. It is a *medical* welfare program for people with less than $1500 in countable assets other than their home, an irrevocable burial account, and one car. Each state governs the allocation of available funds. Be advised, however, that when the surviving spouse dies and the house is sold, the state may seek reimbursement. This only applies to certain people on Medicaid.

If you want information about Medicaid, call the Department of Human Services, which is listed in the government section of your phone book under the county in which you live.

SSI: Social Security Insurance (SSI) is a government-sponsored *payment* program administered by Social Security for people with inadequate income and who are blind, physically disabled, or over 65. SSI provides supplemental income for those who did not work long enough to qualify for full social security benefits.

OAA: If you have a financial need, your best resource may be contacting a government agency listed in your phone book under Area Agency on Aging. It is part of the Older Americans Act (OAA) of 1965 which was reauthorized in 1992, providing many services for citizens with very limited income. Each state controls its own program.

Family and Medical Leave Act: The Family and Medical Leave Act of 1993 (FMLA) entitles some employees to take up to twelve weeks per year of unpaid leave to help take care of a spouse or parent who is seriously ill. There are many details and stipulations to this act, however, and they should be checked if you have need to consider it.

Information may be obtained from the Internet, or you may contact the nearest office of the Wage and Hour Division listed in most telephone directories under U.S. Government, Department of Labor. Written correspondence may be sent to the following address: U.S. Department of Labor, Employment Standards Administration, Wage and Hour Division, Washington, DC 20210.

The Internet also lists several other social and government agencies that might be helpful. If you do not have a computer with Internet capability, your library can help you with this. You may also find listings in your phone book under the Federal Government heading.

Chapter 22

When Death Occurs

For those who do not have hospice service when a loved one dies, community paramedics may be called. Some attendants are qualified as "skilled observers" and may be able to pronounce your loved one as deceased and notify the doctor. Otherwise the ambulance must stop at the hospital emergency room for pronouncement before going to the funeral home. Medicare, Medicaid, and most personal insurance policies cover this expense.

If you call the funeral home directly, the attendants who come to your home to transport the deceased may be qualified as "skilled observers." They can make arrangements to notify the coroner if necessary.

Coping with Emotions

Don't be ashamed or afraid to show your grief. This catharsis is important to your future well-being; it will help to give closure to the past and adjustment to the future.

Guilt feelings: Occasionally after a loved one dies, there are feelings of guilt that perhaps everything possible (either medically or emotionally) wasn't done. You can probably think of *something* you wish you had done differently. Concede that you did the best you could at the time you did it.

Sometimes people will experience unrealistic guilt over situations in which they have no control. This type of guilt is irrational and needs to be discussed. If you are having these feelings, you may want to talk about them with a close friend or perhaps your pastor or funeral director. They are usually sympathetic listeners.

Be aware that guilt, whether normal or irrational, may be harmful physically and mentally if not resolved. Often the arranging of a meaningful funeral or memorial service can redirect a grieving person's feelings into something positive and uplifting.

Medication: As much as possible, avoid medication such as sedatives. Although drugs may provide some needed relief, they should not be taken just to avoid the reality of grief. A period of grief is needed to make the adjustment to healthy living.

Accept people's care: If you have children, family, or friends who can help to ease the hurt for you, let them envelop you with their love. They may not know what to say or do to express their compassion, but allow their attempts to help fill the void you are feeling.

Friends may not understand how comforting it is for you to talk about your loved one; if they seem reluctant to do it, explain your desire to them. Do not be afraid to cry. Crying at this time is a normal reaction, and it is better to release tensions and feelings than to lock them up inside.

Allow yourself to be cared for at this time. Others can help you with the myriad of small details that demand attention. No matter how well prepared you may be, there is still much to be done. Permitting your family and friends to take over as much as they can will relieve you of the burden and help them cope with their own stress and grief.

Natural fears: You may find it difficult to concentrate on anything. You may voice to yourself or to others, "What is wrong with me?

What am I going to do?" You may even fear that you are losing control and worry about your own stability. If you feel panic encroaching, take some deep breaths, talk to friends (or perhaps your pastor), and realize that the Lord is in charge of your tomorrows as well as your today.

Normal adjustments: Laughter *will* come again, and it's important that you embrace it. Don't feel guilty the first time you laugh again—even if it is during this time of deep sorrow and grief. Laughter, like tears, can be an emotional release, and your loved one would be pleased to know you are adjusting to life.

Realize that your children or other family members may react differently to their grief than you do to yours. Give them this freedom and be understanding. Recognize that each person deals with grief individually. Some may choose to shut themselves up in a room and grieve alone, while others may find release by being gregarious and laughing. Those who don't cry may hurt just as much as those who do, and you may need to encourage family members to be tolerant of each other.

Handling resentment: If you have friends whose mates are still living, you may find yourself being resentful (or jealous) of their happiness. If you are still working, you may resent other employees who are planning their retirements with their loved ones when you have none to anticipate with your loved one.

Remembering the good times you had with your loved one will help bridge the gap to happiness. Good memories in particular can be a bountiful blessing, one which many people have never been privileged to have. Making your own plans for the future can also help remedy resentment over prospects of a lonely retirement. Concentrate on what you have, not what you don't have, and use those resources to their fullest. See your situation not as what it is but as what it can become with God's help.

You may even have resentment toward your loved one if health issues (such as smoking or heavy alcohol consumption) were ignored and caused this pain for you. Remember, instead, the many good qualities your loved one had.

Practical Advice

The first few days and weeks after the death of a loved one are usually the most difficult. Some people, however, have said that three or four months later is the hardest time. That is when friends and relatives have returned to their own lifestyles, and life seems especially lonely for you.

For me, being busy and active helped, but for you this may not offer relief. We are all different in how we cope with loneliness and how we face the future. One of my friends *wanted* to be alone.

In talking with several others who have lost their mates, the following suggestions surfaced. Perhaps they will be helpful for you.

Clothing disposal: Disposing of a loved one's clothing is perhaps the most difficult thing that has to be done. Some prefer to do it right away, and others would rather wait. One woman found comfort with the clothing still in the closet, as if her husband had gone away for just a short time and would return. When she did finally dispose of the clothing, she kept back several things that evoked special memories.

It may be better, however, to give everything away and make a clean break to your "new life." I gave all of Bob's clothes to a local rescue mission. This gave me comfort knowing the clothes could be used to help someone else.

Eating alone: You may find yourself still getting out two plates, two saucers, and two cups at mealtime. Old habits are not easily broken, but don't let that alarm you. For me, one of the most difficult encounters was seeing just one chair on the patio extension instead of two. To remedy this, I put out a second chair and gave it to the Lord. In Isaiah 54:5, the Bible tells us the Lord is the husband of widows.

Empty bedroom: The most haunting room in your house may be your bedroom—with the bed that remains empty on one side. One woman found comfort in placing a picture of her husband on the vacant pillow. Another woman purchased an electric blanket so the unoccupied side of the bed would be warm. One other woman sprinkled the covers with her husband's cologne.

For some, remodeling the bedroom was the answer to starting a new chapter in life. One woman purchased more modern furniture and a new twin-size bed.

Cemetery visit: Going to the cemetery was comforting for some; being at the grave site rendered a sense of closeness with their departed loved one. One woman brought fresh flowers to her husband's grave each week, and sometimes she would linger a long time and sing their favorite hymns. For others, going to the cemetery was difficult. Though returning to the grave the first time after the funeral is traumatic, it helps the healing.

Nostalgic places: Some have found pleasure in returning to places that were especially meaningful to them and their loved ones. One woman relived a trip through Virginia on the Skyline Drive that had been a happy time of vacationing. For others, a familiar place was like a probe opening up fresh tissue in a healing wound, and they found the experience to be painful.

Functioning alone: Going to social activities alone may be difficult. It may be hard to go to church, sit in a pew by yourself, or attend a couples' Sunday school class. Reaching out to others helps, and each time the venture becomes easier.

If friends (especially couples) invite you to do things with them, don't feel you are butting into their lives. Try to realize they wouldn't ask if they didn't want to be with you.

Friends help bridge the gap to a fulfilling life, and a special friendship with another person who likewise is alone can be rewarding. Sharing your thoughts openly and relating problems and memories help to alleviate emotional pain.

Support groups: Joining a support group may be helpful. Our local hospice has one that meets monthly and invites community leaders to speak on relevant subjects. Most cities have local AARP chapters, which sponsor a Widowed Persons Service. This may include support meetings, telephone service, or outreach on a personal basis. (Please see Chapter 24, "Helpful Organizations.")

Some support groups get together just to talk and share concerns. Often funeral homes can recommend such a group. There are also support groups for children or grandchildren if they have difficulty coping with the death.

Many churches also sponsor similar programs. If there is no support group of any kind available in your community, you might want to help others by starting one.

Pets: For some, a pet helps alleviate loneliness. An excited, tail-wagging puppy that is always glad to see you can ease the feeling of isolation. Or a loving cat that is content to rest on your lap and purr while you watch TV can be a great comfort.

Time with God: For me, spending time with the Lord was helpful, although others found reading the Bible to be difficult (a devotional guide helps). One woman said she couldn't pray for several days after her husband's death, but when she couldn't fashion her own words, she found strength in repeating the Lord's Prayer (Matthew 6:9-13).

Renew activities: It's important that you become involved with life again. (I am sure your loved one would want it that way.) For me, returning to church activities was stimulating, and reaching out to other people helped put me back into the mainstream of life. I found one of my greatest blessings was to know I was needed.

Serve others: Concentrating on serving others and developing new interests will help to relieve loneliness and give life new purpose. You may want to become involved in community projects. Volunteers are sorely needed in many areas, depending on individual interests. The

Garden Club can always use more help. I have a friend who is involved with a civic theater. Agencies such as pregnancy centers and youth organizations might be a welcome challenge.

Becoming involved with Habitat for Humanity or signing up for a short tenure as an overseas missionary might appeal to the more adventuresome. The AARP Volunteer Talent Bank matches potential volunteers with suitable volunteer positions based on identified interests, skills, and geographic location.

Perhaps your niche of service is helping your family. Baby-sitting with grandchildren has been a rewarding option for many.

Job considerations: If you are interested in a job change or a different career, Intercristo Christian Placement Network (1-800-426-1342 or 1-800-251-7740; www.jobleads.org on the Internet) introduces people to organizations that can use their particular talents, for a small charge. AARP also offers counseling services. (See Chapter 24 for Displaced Homemaker's Network.)

Further education: Pursing further education might be a viable choice, or increasing involvement at work could spark an interest for anyone still employed. Joining a travel club or a theater group could add a new dimension to anyone's life.

Identity crisis: Finding one's own identity after a mate's death may be a great challenge. A woman, in particular, may feel her chief role in life was to be her husband's mate—everyone knows her as "Joe's wife"—and now she must take over the control of her existence. If identity is a problem, remember that God loves you, and He will indeed "strengthen you and uplift you." *You* are important to Him, and with His help, you can do whatever is needed to find your own identity.

Delay decisions: Almost everyone agrees—make no major decisions—such as selling a home and moving in with one of the children—for at least a year. Immediately taking a trip is not the answer either. Learning to cope with your loss is important, and running away will not help.

Instead of quitting a job, take a leave of absence; rent the house out instead of selling it; visit the family for a week or two instead of deciding to move in with them.

Also, avoid making any serious financial changes until you have had time to secure help from a qualified adviser.

Health concerns: Above all, take care of yourself. Try to eat a balanced diet and resist the temptation of just snacking. Moderate exercise, too, is important. Mental, emotional, and spiritual health are essential. Accepting each day as a gift from God can be helpful, realizing life *can* be lived to its fullest potential even after the death of a loved one.

Legal Considerations

Among the legal things that need to be done, the will must be filed in probate court. This can be done by a lawyer who will give you advice regarding other legal tasks such as payment of taxes (or tax release), filing insurance claims, etc. A copy of the death certificate is needed for each transaction.

Social Security: If your loved one has paid into social security for at least forty quarters, you are eligible for survivor's benefits if you are age 60 or older. (Disabled widows or widowers age 50 or older are eligible.) Since rules change frequently, check with a local office regarding your individual needs. By calling Social Security's toll-free number (1-800-772-1213), you can speak to a service representative during normal business hours. Those with touch-tone phones have the availability of recorded information about services on evenings, weekends, and holidays.

Social Security requires the following information: marriage certificate (available at the office of the county clerk where the license was issued), copies of birth certificates for dependent children (available at either state or county public health offices where children were born), spouse's birth certificate, death certificate, military discharge papers, social security card, and copies of deceased's most recent federal income tax return. Social Security also pays a death benefit of $255 toward burial expenses.

Estate tax: Since 1987, a federal estate tax is due only on estates exceeding $600,000. The tax return must be filed (Form 706 from the IRS), and taxes must be paid within nine months of date of death. State laws regarding taxes differ. For details, consult the state tax or revenue department usually listed in the government section of the telephone directory. 2002 - EXCEEDING #1,000,000.

Probate: State laws differ regarding probate, the legal process of paying the deceased's debts and distributing the estate to rightful heirs. The lawyer usually handles this; otherwise consult the probate court. Proceeds from a life insurance policy or IRA that are paid directly to a beneficiary are not subject to probate.

Chapter 23

Miscellaneous Concerns

Perhaps the suggestions listed below will help you focus on your present need regarding your loved one. You may want to put a check mark beside each item as you consider it.

People to Contact

Names, addresses, and phone numbers of the following:

Employer
Attorney
Accountant
Broker
Insurance agent(s)
Executor
Bank(s)

Death Certificate Information

In some states the names of the decedent's father and mother (including maiden name) are required for the death certificate. Other necessary information may include:

Social Security number
Date and place of birth
Branch of armed forces (if decedent was in armed forces)
Usual occupation (type of business or industry)
Race
Education (number of college years specified)

Important Papers

Important papers should be designated—what they are and where they may be located:

Will
Insurance policies
Deeds
Mortgages
Tax returns
Receipts
Warranties
Miscellaneous documents: birth and marriage certificates,
    diplomas, military papers, etc.

Other Helpful Information

Credit cards listed by issuer and number
Car registration, insurance, and loan information
Homeowner records: taxes, liens, and leases
Safe deposit box: location of key and contents defined
Debts or loans listed: terms, payments or collateral
Trusts: type, size, name and address of trustee
Stocks and bonds: certificate numbers, issuer and location
Savings account passbooks and checkbooks
Location of canceled checks and statements

Personal Information

The following facts might be needed for an obituary or memorial service:

Schools attended or degrees earned
Past employment
Social, business, or military accomplishments
Past marital relationships
Children (perhaps by a previous marriage)
Other noteworthy relatives (living or deceased)
Relatives to notify (perhaps out of town or country)

If you are not certain about any of this information regarding your loved one, ask questions. Are you *sure* you know the location of all important papers and what they mean? (My attorney recommends that wills and other legal papers be kept in a safety deposit box.)

Chapter 24

Helpful Organizations

This is a list of some of the national organizations that may provide help for you.

■ American Brain Tumor Association
2720 River Road, Suite 146, Des Plaines, IL 60018 (847-827-9910, 1-800-886-2282)
This organization offers printed materials about research and treatment of brain tumors and provides resource listings of physicians, treatment facilities, and support groups throughout the country.

■ American Cancer Society
1599 Clifton Road NE, Atlanta, GA 30329 (404-320-3333, 1-800-227-2345)
The ACS is a volunteer organization offering a variety of services to patients and their families. It supports research, provides printed materials, and conducts educational programs. Local ACS units are listed in the white pages under "American Cancer Society."

■ Bloch National Cancer Hot Line (1-800-433-0464)
Sponsored by the R. A. Bloch Cancer Foundation, this hot line was started in 1990 by Richard A. Bloch and his wife, Annette. It is a

special service in which newly diagnosed cancer patients may talk with individuals who have been successfully treated for their type of cancer. Volunteers offer hope to new patients and help them discover their best treatment options.

■ The Cancer Information Service (1-800-422-6237)
The CIS, a program of the National Cancer Institute, provides a nationwide telephone service for cancer patients and their families, the public, and health-care professionals. CIS information specialists have extensive training in providing up-to-date and understandable information about cancer and cancer research. CIS offices serve specific geographic areas and have information about cancer-related services and resources in their region. Free printed material is available.

■ The Displaced Homemaker's Network
1625 K Street NW, Suite 300, Washington, DC 20006
(202-467-6346)
    This network can tell you where the nearest career counseling center is located and help with a return to the job market.

■ Federal Information Center (1-800-688-9889)
This toll-free number can give you information on a variety of government services ranging from tax information to job availability. This is a good first number to call for any type of government help.

■ Hospice Education Institute
190 Westbrook Road, Suite 3-B, Essex, CT 06426 (1-800-331-1620; in Alaska and Connecticut, 860-767-1620)
    The Hospice Education Institute offers information about hospice care and can refer cancer patients and their families to local hospice programs.

■ The International THEOS Foundation (THEOS)
322 Boulevard of the Allies, Suite 105, Pittsburgh, PA 15222-1919
(412-471-7779)

This is an international support network for recently widowed men and women through over 120 local chapters. They offer monthly meetings and one-on-one support services to help participants work through their immediate grief and cope with day-to-day practical concerns. Many local chapters are sponsored by religious congregations and funeral homes. Numerous publications are available, including the magazine *Survivor's Outreach.*

■ Last Acts Coalition/Burness Communications
7910 Woodmont Ave., Suite 1340, Bethesda MD 20814
(301-652-1558)
Former First Lady Rosalynn Carter is honorary chair of "Last Acts," which is a coalition of seventy-two prominent organizations (including clergy, consumer groups, hospice organizations, and voluntary organizations like the Alzheimer's Association and the American Cancer Society) for improving the quality of care for dying patients. They address issues related to family needs, health-care providers, education and training, and palliative care.

■ Leukemia Society of America
600 Third Avenue, Fourth Floor, New York, NY 10016
(1-800-955-4572—publications only)
The LSA is concerned with leukemia, lymphoma, and related diseases. It supports research and provides printed materials. It also offers financial assistance and provides information about other resources for patients and their families. Further information is available by calling a local chapter listed in the white pages of the telephone directory.

■ Mayo Clinic Health Oasis (www.mayohealth.org)
News and links that are organized into nine categories, including cancer, medicine, and nutrition. Visitors can E-mail questions to Mayo doctors.

■ National Association for Home Care
228 Seventh Street SE, Washington, DC 20002 (202-547-7424)
This organization offers information about home health-care services. The association offers a free brochure, *How to Select a Home Health Agency.*

■ National Coalition for Cancer Survivorship
1010 Wayne Avenue, Suite 505, Silver Spring, MD 20910
(1-888-937-6227)
This network of groups and individuals offers support to cancer survivors and their loved ones. It provides information and resources on support and life following a cancer diagnosis.

■ National Hospice Organization
1901 North Moore Street, Suite 901, Arlington, VA 22209
(703-243-5900—publications line; 1-800-658-8898—referrals only).
The National Hospice Organization is an association of groups that provide hospice care. It promotes and maintains hospice care and encourages support for patients and family members. Information about hospice concepts is also available.

■ National Marrow Donor Program
3433 Broadway Street NE, Suite 500, Minneapolis, MN 55413
(612-627-5800, 1-800-627-7692)
Funded by the federal government, this organization keeps a registry of potential bone-marrow donors and provides a free packet of information on bone-marrow transplantation.

■ OncoLink (www.oncolink.com)
A source of information about specific cancers and treatments, clinical trials, and support groups. Information ranges from the basic to the highly technical.

■ Radio Bible Class, RBC Ministries, Grand Rapids, MI 49555-0001
(616-942-6770, 1-800-598-7221)
Many helpful booklets and pamphlets written from the Christian

viewpoint are available through RBC Ministries. If you call or write, they will send a list of available publications.

■ Skin Cancer Foundation
245 Fifth Avenue, Suite 1403, New York, NY 10016
(212-725-5176, 1-800-754-6490)
    This organization conducts public- and medical-education programs to help reduce skin cancer. It seeks to increase public awareness of the importance of taking protective measures against the damaging rays of the sun and to teach people how to recognize the early signs of skin cancer.

■ Social Security Information (1-800-772-1213)
You may obtain answers to most Social Security questions by calling this number. They will provide local numbers for information relevant to particular states.

■ United Ostomy Association
19772 MacArthur Blvd, Suite 200, Irvine, CA 92612-2405
(949-660-8624, 1-800-826-0826; 7:30 A.M. - 4:30 P.M. PST)
    This organization helps ostomy patients through mutual aid and emotional support. It provides information to patients and the public and sends volunteers to visit with new ostomy patients.

■ Widowed Persons Service (AARP)
601 E. Street NW, Washington, DC 20049 (202-434-2260)
    This arm of AARP is specifically devoted to helping widows and widowers. It is a rich resource for a variety of helpful booklets. If you call or write, they will send a list of available publications.

PART THREE

Recommended Reading

Inspirational Reading:

- Canfield, Jack, with Mark Victor Hansen, Patty Aubrey, and Nancy Mitchell. *Chicken Soup for the Surviving Soul.* Deerfield Beach, Fla.: Health Communications, 1996.

  This book is a compilation of 101 stories of people who have *survived* cancer, and it is lighthearted reading that anyone might find uplifting. It embraces topics such as hope, courage, faith, and love.

- Dravecky, Jan, with Connie Neal. *A Joy I'd Never Known.* Grand Rapids, Mich.: Zondervan Publishing House, 1996.

  Jan Dravecky, wife of Dave Dravecky, the star pitcher for the San Francisco Giants who lost his pitching arm to cancer, shares Dave's triumphs and his tragedy. After his surgery she struggled with an aching heart and depression. When she released control of her life to a loving God, she found the real joy of living. Her life story and the lessons she learned will reassure you that you, too, can find answers you may be seeking.

- Elliot, Elisabeth. *A Path Through Suffering.* Ann Arbor, Mich.: Servant Publications, 1992.

  The subtitle of the book is *Discovering the Relationship between God's Mercy and Our Pain.* Comprised of short vignettes that can be read quickly, it is a powerfully moving book that tenderly examines personal hurts.

- Elliot, Elisabeth. *Keep a Quiet Heart.* Ann Arbor, Mich.: Servant Publications, 1995.

This book is a collection of short articles that provide a unique, interesting way to teach us more about God.

- Gill, A. L. *God's Promises for Your Every Need.* Dallas: Word Publishing, 1995.

This book offers help in claiming God's blessings for your life. It will point you to Scripture that will bolster your spirits and lift discouragement, worry, and fear. It will reassure you of God's love and forgiveness through His many promises.

- Gray, Alice. *Stories for the Heart.* Sisters, Ore.: Multnomah Publishers, 1996.

Alice Gray has compiled 110 stories that will add a little joy to your life and encourage your soul. Max Lucado, James Dobson, Kay Arthur, Billy Graham, and Chuck Swindoll are among the book's contributors. Some of the stories are short, but as you visit with them—even if only for a few fleeting minutes—they will warm your heart and brighten your day.

- Hawkins, Don. *Never Give Up: The Incredible Payoff of Perseverance.* Lincoln, Nebr.: Back to the Bible Broadcast, 1992.

Instead of reciting empty platitudes and promises, the author takes a realistic approach to living confidently in the face of life's greatest difficulties. As a pastor for almost two decades, he offers a biblical foundation for hope and encouragement.

- Shropshire, Marie. *In Touch with God.* Eugene, Ore.: Harvest House, 1985.

With the subtitle of *How God Speaks to a Prayerful Heart,* the book is written as a conversation with the Lord. The author asks questions about sorrow, guilt, loneliness, and other emotions that haunt those who have lost a loved one, and God gives kind and understanding answers. This beautiful book could give you much comfort.

- Swindoll, Charles R. *The Grace Awakening.* Dallas: Word Publishing, 1996.
  This is an excellent resource if you would like to explore God's grace in more detail. It describes what grace is, how it is given, and what hindrances there are to it. It is an in-depth book with many biblical references.

Devotional Reading:

- *Daily Guideposts.* Carmel, NY: Guideposts Associates, Inc., 1990.
  This yearly book is written by several authors. Each day includes a one-line biblical reference and an uplifting vignette, as well as a short prayer.

- *Today in the Word.* Chicago: Moody Bible Institute.
  This monthly published booklet contains day-by-day personal stories illustrating biblical truths. It may be ordered by writing to Moody Bible Institute or calling 1-800-356-6639.

- *Upper Room Magazine.* Nashville, Tenn.: Board of Discipleship.
  This is a seventy-two-page booklet published monthly. To order a subscription, call 1-800-925-6847.

Books Related to Cancer:

- Anderson, Greg. *Fifty Essential Things to Do When the Doctor Says It's Cancer.* New York: Penguin Books, 1993.
  In 1984 the author was diagnosed with lung cancer at age 37 and given thirty days to live. He studied how other cancer patients had survived their illness, and he patterned his response after theirs. He recovered, and he now shares what he learned so others suffering with cancer may benefit.

- Anderson, Greg, *The Triumphant Patient.* Nashville, Tenn.: Thomas Nelson, 1992.

  This is a parable of a cancer patient who seeks a cure for her illness and, in doing so, discovers how to live a triumphant life. She finds that anger, despair, and hopelessness can be replaced with hope, and a fulfilling and exceptional life, even in illness. As she discovered, cancer can be conquered—even if it isn't cured.

- Burkett, Larry, and Michael E. Taylor. *Damaged But Not Broken.* Chicago: Moody Press, 1996.

  Larry Burkett candidly tells of his battle with cancer and discusses alternative cancer treatments.

- Caring for the Patient with Cancer at Home: A Guide for Patients and Families. This pamphlet from the American Cancer Society might be helpful if your loved one suffers from cancer. It offers instruction on how to administer injections and give tube feedings, and how to care for intravenous lines and oxygen equipment.

- Dravecky, Dave, with Connie W. Neal. *The Worth of a Man.* Grand Rapids, Mich.: Zondervan Publishing House, 1996.

  When Dave Dravecky lost his left arm to cancer, he also lost his career as star pitcher for the San Francisco Giants. Readers can benefit from the author's insights into suffering and the deeper meaning of life.

- Frahm, Anne E., with David J. Frahm. *A Cancer Battle Plan.* New York: The Putnam Publishing Group, 1998.

  After surgery, radiation, chemotherapy, and a bone-marrow transplant, Anne Frahm was given a hopeless prognosis. Then she discovered the connection between cancer and nutrition. After five weeks of a comprehensive nutritional battle plan, her cancer disappeared without a trace. Her book is about that battle plan. It may be ordered from the Christian ministry of Family Life Today (1-800-358-6329).

■ Gullo, Shirley M., Elaine Glass (Editor), and Maria Gamiere (Editor). *Silver Linings: The Other Side of Cancer.* Oncology Nursing Press, Inc., 1997.

Written by two oncology nurses, this book is a heartwarming collection of inspirational stories, poetry and quotes from cancer survivors, their families, and friends. If not available in bookstores, it may be ordered from the Oncology Nursing Society at 1-412-921-7373.

■ Harwell, Amy. *Ready to Live, Prepared to Die.* Wheaton, Ill.: Harold Shaw Publishers, 1995.

Part workbook, part guidebook, part personal survival story, this book makes an excellent guide in preparations for both living and dying. The author covers such issues as heroic resuscitation, suicide, funerals, unfinished business, forgiveness, blessings, and saying good-byes.

■ Salaman, Maureen. *Nutrition: The Cancer Answer.* Menlo Park, Calif.: M K S, Inc., 1983.

The preventative approach to combating cancer is the central theme of this book. It emphasizes the importance of good nutrition and gives several recipes and suggestions to help implement it.

Books Relating to Suffering:

■ Hill, Nancy. *Living with Terminal Illness.* St. Louis, Mo.: Concordia Publishing House, 1996.

This small book is part of the *Master's Touch Bible* study books. Although it is designed for group Bible study, the questions asked and issues addressed might also be helpful in individual study.

■ Lockyer, Herbert. *Dark Threads the Weaver Needs.* Ada, Mich.: Fleming H. Revell, 1996.

This book addresses the questions we ask when suffering from pain, difficulty, or sorrow: "Why me? Why is this happening? Why is God silent?" The author assures readers that the comfort of God,

Christ, the Spirit, Scripture, and other believers will console them in their suffering until the time comes when they will suffer no more.

- MacArthur, John. *The Power of Suffering.* Colorado Springs, Colo.: Chariot Victor Publishing, 1995.

The author examines the reality of pain and trials in the Christian life and, from a pastor's heart, offers a plausible, thoroughly biblical explanation for the deep valleys each of us inevitably encounters. Also included is a six-step Bible study regarding suffering.

Books Dealing with Grief:

- Lynn, Carol. *A Time to Grieve.* Uhrichsville, Ohio: Barbour Publishing, 1995.

This little book can conveniently fit into a purse for easy reference. Written in conversational style, it gives help and hope from the Bible. The author describes the stages of grief and shares poignant examples from her own life of how to deal with the devastating emotions.

- Sissom, Ruth. *Moving Beyond Grief.* Grand Rapids, Mich.: Discovery House Publishers, 1994.

This book contains sixteen intimate, first-person stories written by men and women whose lives were touched by death. Some lost spouses; others lost children or other family members. Each one shares the struggles encountered and the victories achieved over grief, loneliness, fear, and frustration. It is an uplifting book that will enhance your courage.

- Westberg, Granger E. *Good Grief.* Minneapolis, Minn.: Augsburg Fortress Publishers, 1962.

Many people have found this book to be helpful. It gently discusses ten stages of grief and offers subtle advice for each one.

Books about Heaven:

- Graham, Billy. *Angels.* Dallas: Word Publishing, 1995.

With the backing of Scripture, Dr. Graham describes the many aspects of angels from being "invisible hosts" to "ministering servants." This comforting book describes angels' function in times past, in this present era, and in the age to come.

- Lockyer, Herbert. *Dying, Death, & Destiny.* Ada, Mich.: Fleming H. Revell, 1996.

  In a book that is warm and compassionate, Dr. Lockyer presents a heartfelt portrait of death as the great leveler of humanity. He laces it with assurance, hope, and spiritual significance as he discusses heaven and hell and the reality of both.

- Lucado, Max. *The Applause of Heaven.* Dallas: Word Publishing, 1996.

  In a relaxed, conversational style, the author brings the Beatitudes into modern-day life. He illustrates each one with intimate stories about biblical characters and living people. The last chapter encompasses heaven—but by then you know what it means to be there.

- MacArthur, John. *The Glory of Heaven.* Wheaton, Ill.: Crossway Books, 1996.

  In this book the author takes the reader through passages of Scripture that open up the realities of heaven, angels, and eternal life. With scholarly attention, he describes "what heaven will be like" and "what we will be like in heaven." The book also includes sermons by such famous theologians as Charles H. Spurgeon and J. C. Ryle.

- Stowell, Joseph M. *Eternity.* Chicago: Moody Press, 1997.

  When tragedy strikes or death seems inevitable, the question of where we will spend eternity becomes vital. Dr. Stowell weaves biblical references with real-life stories to give a compassionate insight into the realities of heaven. He also addresses problems of daily living before eternity.

■ Tada, Joni Eareckson. *Heaven: Your Real Home.* Grand Rapids, Mich.: Zondervan Publishing House, 1997.

Joni Eareckson Tada's book gives a beautiful picture of that glorious destination awaiting all believers when the trials of earth are finished. In language that is easy to understand, it answers such questions as Where is heaven and what is it like? What will we do in heaven?

Books for Children on Death and Dying:

■ Nystrom, Carolyn. *What Happens When We Die?* Chicago: Moody Press, 1998.

This small hardback has a scriptural basis, but it answers questions about death in a child's language.

■ O'Connor, Joey. *Heaven's Not a Crying Place.* Ada, Mich.: Fleming H. Revell, 1997

Tough questions about death and funerals often push parents out of their comfort zone. This is a sensitive, compassionate book that gently gives advice on how to teach children about death within the larger scope of life.

Miscellaneous Books:

■ Carter, Rosalynn, and Susan K. Golant. *Helping Yourself Help Others.* New York: Random House, Inc., 1996.

As you face the prospect of caregiving, this book by our former First Lady Rosalyn Carter may be very helpful. It is an excellent resource for the care of many types of disabilities, ranging from cancer to kidney disease. Resources include organizations, hot lines, and related reading.

■ Chapin, Alice. *Reaching Back.* Cincinnati, Ohio: F & W Publications, Inc., 1996.

This is a workbook for recording life's most meaningful moments that may be shared with future generations. There is room for pictures and newspaper clippings.

■ *Guideposts.* Carmel, N.Y.: Guideposts Associates, Inc.

This nondenominational monthly is spiritually uplifting and small enough to fit in a woman's purse. The articles are short and poignant, true stories of ordinary people who have been touched by God. Each story has an encouraging take-away, a conclusion that will brighten your day and strengthen your faith.

■ Lashier, Kathleen. *Mom, Share Your Life with Me.* Waverly, Iowa: G & R Publishing, 1992.

Kathleen Lashier has written a series in the form of a diary, evoking a different memory for each day in the year. Additional titles include *Dad, Share Your Life with Me; Granddad, Tell Me Your Memories;* and *Grandma, Tell Me Your Memories.*

These books elicit answers to such questions as What did you do on your first date? What do you remember as your favorite subject in school? What was the best vacation you ever had? By the time the book is finished, words have painted the picture of your life and brought your personal history to life.

■ McDonald, Mary Lynne. *The Christian's Guide to Money Matters for Women.* Grand Rapids, Mich.: Zondervan Publishing House, 1995.

If your loved one has left you with stocks or other financial investments, you may find this book helpful. Mary Lynne McDonald, who is a certified financial planner, writes in an easy-to-understand style. Her advice ranges from refinancing the mortgage on a home to establishing a budget. She suggests fifty-five ways to save money.

■ Moon, Marilyn, and Janemarie Mulvey. *Entitlements & the Elderly.* Washington, D.C.: Urban Institute Press, 1995.

This book discusses the major entitlements that protect the elderly: Social Security, Medicare, and Medicaid.

■ Sprinkle, Patricia H. *Women Home Alone.* Grand Rapids, Mich.: Zondervan Publishing House, 1996.

Facing life alone can be frightening, but Sprinkle's book can be very helpful. It addresses such problems as finances, leaking faucets, medical emergencies, and major decisions. The author talks to her readers like a next-door neighbor. She reaches into her own experiences and those of others to give practical, upbeat, hands-on guidance for self-sufficiency. She draws on insights from carpenters, police officers, mechanics, financial advisers, and other professionals. It is a book well worth having.

■ Yeh, Elizabeth. *How to Achieve Quality of Life & Care in a Nursing Home.* Houston, Tex.: Student College Aid, 1995.

In this book, the author, who has degrees in both nursing and social work, discusses different types of facilities, how to choose a nursing home, how to handle the finances, plus questions and answers.

Daily Renewal

Coping with life really does get easier as time distances you from death, but there may always be flashes of pain. Being busy is an antidote, and helping others is the essence of joy.

Look for the good things that come with each new day: the song of a bird, the unexpected call from an out-of-town friend, a card in the mail just when you need it, a remembered phrase or song that touched your heart. Often it is these little things that give life the radiance of a polished jewel.

Just as dough has to be kneaded to produce the wonderful aroma of freshly baked bread, sometimes our lives have to be traumatized to bring out their full potential. Trust God that He is making something beautiful of your life.

Through it all, may our Lord direct your life and give you His peace.

        Your friend,
        Faye Landrum